The Frid Factor

The Frid Factor

A Pragmatic Guide to Building a Knowledge Management Program

Dr. Randy J. Frid

e-mail: dr.frid@frid.com
website: www.decision-matrix.com

Writers Club Press
San Jose New York Lincoln Shanghai

The Frid Factor
A Pragmatic Guide to Building a Knowledge Management Program

Writers Club Press
an imprint of iUniverse, Inc.

For information address:
iUniverse, Inc.
5220 S. 16th St., Suite 200
Lincoln, NE 68512
www.iuniverse.com

Knowledge Management
Business Intelligence

ISBN: 0-595-23138-1

Printed in the United States of America

DEDICATION

This book is dedicated to my wife and kids who have been my adventurous companions as we've traveled far and wide on my quest to advocate KM over the past decade. The road of life takes many strange twists and turns. When the going is good it's usually great, and even when it's not so good, it's at least made bearable if you travel in the right company.

Home is where the heart is, so they say. So if you can travel the world, and take those close to your heart along with you, life is good.

I would also like to thank Deb and Bill, Anita, Betty and Don for everything they have done to help along the way. They're always there for us, making our journey a little easier.

CONTENTS

Common Vocabulary

Throughout this book we will frequently use terminology not common to our daily workplace, so I'll use Merriam-Webster to begin establishing a common vocabulary that we can live with:

tacit

1: expressed or carried on without words or speech
2 a: implied or indicated but not actually expressed <*tacit* consent> b (1): arising without express contract or agreement (2): arising by operation of law <*tacit* mortgage>

explicit

1 a: fully revealed or expressed without vagueness, implication, or ambiguity: leaving no question as to meaning or intent <*explicit* instructions> b: open in the depiction of nudity or sexuality <*explicit* books and films>
2: fully developed or formulated <an *explicit* plan> <an *explicit* notion of our objective>
3: unambiguous in expression <was very *explicit* on how we are to behave>

interpolate

1 a: to alter or corrupt (as a text) by inserting new or foreign matter b: to insert (words) into a text or into a conversation

2: to insert between other things or parts
3: to estimate values of (a function) between two known values
intransitive senses: to make insertions (as of estimated values)

meta

Etymology: New Latin & Medieval Latin, from Latin or Greek; Latin, from Greek, among, with, after, from *meta* among, with, after; akin to Old English *mid, mith* with, Old High German *mit*
1 a: occurring later than or in succession to: after <*metestrus*> b: situated behind or beyond <*metencephalon*> <*metacarpus*> c: later or more highly organized or specialized form of <*metaxylem*>

heuristic

: involving or serving as an aid to learning, discovery, or problem-solving by experimental and especially trial-and-error methods <*heuristic* techniques> <a *heuristic* assumption>; *also*: of or relating to exploratory problem-solving techniques that utilize self-educating techniques (as the evaluation of feedback) to improve performance <a *heuristic* computer program>

lexicon

:A dictionary.
:A stock of terms used in a particular profession, subject, or style; a vocabulary: the lexicon of surrealist art.

ontology

:An explicit formal specification of how to represent the objects, concepts and other entities that are assumed to exist in some area of interest and the relationships that hold among them.

INTRODUCTION

Long, long ago…in a galaxy far, far away….

A few years back I wrote my first book on Knowledge Management. Since then I've had many additional opportunities to implement KM programs for large and small organizations alike.

So I decided it was high time to write another book on knowledge management, only this time I want to break KM down into its constituent parts so it can be implemented and measured a little easier by using a variety of the tools and techniques I've had the opportunity to work with.

I find that when I go to the local bookstore or library, or take a quick walk through the available KM websites, I find volumes of supporting KM literature speaking of cultures, the theory of knowledge and other intangibles. These publications are quite helpful. In fact I have been guilty myself of adding to that body of theory and speculation on occasion.

Although these historical literary works on KM can be of value, I get the sense that anyone reading the bulk of available documentation could possibly have a difficult time translating them into something tangible that will help them deliver their organizations products or services. Theory is great but eventually one has to put it into practice to prove its value.

Therefore, I am devoting this book to taking knowledge management one level deeper than the theory of knowledge, into the next realm of KM Program delivery. I do not intend to spend a great deal of time dwelling on specific products (except for one) because the products change daily, but I will talk about the context in which many of today's technologies (in general) can be utilized.

I really hope to take you, the reader, down from the lofty 50,000-foot view of knowledge management, down to around 10,000-20,000 feet. Any lower than that and I'd never get another consulting gig.

And you say, "If only knowledge management came in a shrink-wrap package like software or cookies."

Well, guess what? It can. Sort of...

I've written this book to help Chief Knowledge Officers (or anyone else for that matter) develop a solid Knowledge Management Program by breaking it down into manageable bite-sized chucks, both the theory and the practice.

Any project, be it a KM project or otherwise, if done without the right tools or knowledge stands a high likelihood of failing. All the tools we need are available to us (with many getting better daily), and so is the knowledge. But before we can build, one must first understand at least the fundamentals of KM theory, but once you understand the nature of KM, then you can focus on implementation. The theory behind KM is basically human psychology and physiology, so it's integrated into our very fabric of existence. So, once we paint the picture on the wall you can rest assured that it will be around for a long, long time.

Therefore, with our KM theory roadmap on the wall for constant reflection, we can basically put it aside and focus on actually building something tangible.

I've kept the book lean because I find big books have a tendency to contain a lot of filler that I just don't think you'll need. If you want case studies there are lots of good books and websites that can give you that type of support material. I find most people in KM are cerebral by nature and can figure out how to fill in the gaps. So I'll give you the framework that I use and you take it from there.

Dr. Randy Frid

But First–Show Me the Money

This section contains hard, fast advice for the uninitiated who are looking to get funding for their KM Program. If you have experience in raising project funding you can move on to the next section.

For the record!

There are an unlimited number of ways a company can spend money (ask my wife, she knows them all). In comparison, there are very few ways to make money in a consistent fashion. When one person has money, everybody else wants it.

In an organization it's the job of some people (accountants) to protect that money. It's the job of other people (executives) to make more money.

Now in comes you, and you have a great idea. You want to deploy knowledge management in the enterprise. Well guess what? Everyone else has a great idea too, and they all want to get their hands on the same money you want.

Who's going to win (if anybody)?

That's simple; just look whom you have to convince to hand over that money.

> ➤ The accountants don't want to give away any of it so you can forget about convincing them.

> ➤ That leaves our executives, who all start with the best of intentions and stars in their eyes, but are slowing being consumed by the dark side of the force (accounting).

So the bottom line is, if your great idea is knowledge management, and you can't figure out how it will make or save money (preferably make money), you're in trouble, because you're up against accountants no matter how you look at it. If you work for a government organization then you want to be looking for significant increases in performance and innovation because government is in the business of delivering programs and services to citizens and money is allocated differently than in commercial organizations.

By now, these executives and accountants have seen far too many PowerPoint slides and articles telling them about the benefits of KM and why knowledge management can't be measured, or how it's the flow of this or the exchange of that and that companies should adopt KM no matter what. Or else!

Time to face facts. This is what executives and accountants think:

> "This organization has grown up without a formal KM infra-structure and KM never required 15% of the annual organiza-tional budget in the past. This organization will, in all likelihood, continue to grow without a formal KM program."

Knowledge management is not for the feint of heart or for the whimsi-cal fancies of philosophers. You are asking for some hard earned cash to build something, something of substance that can show an appreciable return on investment. The people that hold the precious cash you need are neither stupid nor wrong; they are in control. They are well aware of

Dr. Randy J. Frid

a world that has seen literally billions of half-baked ideas consume uncountable wealth. Their own survival depends on investing in ideas that can produce a decent ROI, and in terms of government, deliver the programs and services the citizens demand.

So before you go looking for money with hat in hand, you had better:

1. Figure out if your KM program will make or save (preferably make) money. In government you want to define how you will stimulate innovation and/or increase organizational performance in the delivery of programs and services.
2. How much?
3. When?
4. How?
5. How much will it cost?

If your new KM initiative will only produce marginal amounts of money, savings, innovation or performance, forget it! Go find somewhere better to invest the money. KM programs take a lot of time and hard work to implement and maintain. So before any intelligent organization will make this type of commitment, both in time and money, the ROI has to be better than what they would make putting their money in a savings account at the bank (and chip in an extra 10% for cost of capital).

Remember, your new KM program will likely be classified as high risk because your organization probably doesn't have any internal benchmarks that can show that a project like this is likely to succeed. People will only invest in high risk if there is a potential for high return, or why bother risking the money.

Let's assume then that you have determined that there is a great ROI. Before you head off to the CFO you had better ask yourself the same questions he or she will ask you. Remember, you are just about to walk into the lion's den. Not only that but the CFO is the king of the lions and he eats good ideas for breakfast as part of his daily diet. For you this is a great idea and it only makes sense. For the CFO it is just another idea and wishes it only cost cents.

Up to this point you may have put in a great deal of time working through this idea. Put it behind you. When you go looking for money, the investment of your personal time means nothing. It's cash that counts. If you've never asked for money before, don't tell the potential investor that you will contribute your valuable time if they put up the money. Your time has no value, and cash is king as far as accountants are concerned. Be prepared to sell a vision and back it up.

So, now you're in the "other" corner office, the *second* biggest one. What are you going to tell the CFO?

You: "Hey, I've got a great idea to help people share their knowledge."

CFO: "Share? Why would anyone want to share? Now that you make me think about it, I only share my incidental knowledge but I covet and sell my proprietary knowledge. So do you. That's what makes us valuable. How are you going to convince me or anyone else to "give away" what I know?"

You: "Well, I want to build a system where people can get together and collaborate. We'll put together people with similar interests in a community of practice and have them document their best practices on-line for everyone to use. Then they can take advantage of this shared information to better our overall processes"

CFO: "hmmm…You know, I'm usually the one to define what type of knowledge I'm willing to share and I also determine to whom I'm willing to share it with. So do you. Are you going to tell me now, with whom and when I have to share my knowledge? What's in it for me? What's in it for anyone?"

You: "It's good for the company because we will be capturing new knowledge as an asset of the organization."

CFO: "Really? And how, exactly, are you going to value that asset? Where will it show up on the balance sheet? If it becomes an asset then I should be able to liquidate it and get a portion of my money back, right? Let's forget about all this asset talk, I'll figure out what an asset is and isn't."

You: "hmmm…"
You: "hmmm…"
You: "I think we can cut exploratory drilling costs by 50%."

CFO: "I'm listening…"

Set your measure of success up front. If it's attractive and fits the organizational mission, you're usually well received.

As an alternative, and often much simpler way of finding smaller funding, you could go visit your CIO. Most KM initiatives have a significant IT component anyway so you'll be bending a more sympathetic ear (and one with a significant existing budget). The CIO will usually have several IT projects planned and you can often piggyback on one of those. Try squeezing the CIO for the extra 10% contingency money he or she usually budgets into every project. You'll also have a much easier time getting your KM program imbedded into the workflow if you are part of another project. This is another great reason to make your KM programs tactical instead of strategic (as I will discuss later in the book).

Good luck treasure hunting.

Chapter 1–The Background of KM

In my first book "Infrastructure for Knowledge Management" ISBN 0595090532, (the technology parts are dated, but the theory will remain sound for many generations) I speak in-depth on the meaning of knowledge, team building and Knowledge Workers. I will include multiple excerpts here that are still alive and well and living at the heart of KM.

Defining Knowledge Management

Knowledge Management means many things to many people. The term Knowledge Management has been represented from specific products to complete systems but seems to be referenced mostly from the technological perspective. People continue to ask, "What product should we choose?" and the all-time classic, "We're doing knowledge management. We have Lotus Notes".

Well, in one way they're right, and in another way they're wrong.

They're right because we do take advantage of technology to enhance communications and the sharing of knowledge. They are also wrong because they don't really get the point, so they usually only hit on solving part of the problem, which in turn can create other problems.

So what is Knowledge Management?

Simply stated:

Knowledge Management is the application of Processes and Technologies to support the Frid Decision-Cycle

So what is the Frid Decision-Cycle? That's coming up in the next chapter, but for now, let's just say that the Frid Decision-Cycle is the way people think and interact when they make decisions.

Technology can and does play a part in today's knowledge management efforts but the heart and soul of knowledge management must be made very clear at this point. The Frid Decision-Cycle is everything, and from that generates our requirements for knowledge management. Once you understand the Frid Decision-Cycle, everything else just comes in stride, because the objectives, the processes, and the technologies suddenly all begin to make sense.

The Meaning of "Knowledge"

Let's start by giving you some of that nasty theory stuff I spoke of earlier and clarify the meaning of knowledge. This way you can read the first few chapters and never buy another book on KM theory again (except my first book of course).

The idea of Knowledge has been debated for centuries. Plato described it in earliest terms in "The Republic" as being a State of Mind. I believe, at this point in time, that knowledge would be better described as being a State of Certification.

Knowledge can be categorized in two ways:

   1. Tacit (requires us to interpret information and apply judgment)

2. Explicit (enough certification to remove doubt and the need to interpret)

Tacit knowledge is largely opinion-based and deemed conjectural, based on partial or limited evidence and unqualified interpolative data. There is always insufficient supporting evidence to remove doubt in Tacit knowledge.

Explicit knowledge is fact and is qualified with adequate supporting evidence and context that demonstrates enough reconciliation to remove doubt.

All knowledge must also be weighed in its current context. Consider that Explicit knowledge may provide enough evidence to remove doubt, but the evidence may only be supportive under specific circumstances. Changing the context may change a fact to an opinion or an opinion into supposition. As an example, consider the color yellow.

A yellow Volkswagen beetle would be deemed yellow if you maintained a similar velocity with the car. If you were to accelerate the car near the speed of light then you would deem the car to be green if it was traveling towards you, as the light would shift towards the blue spectrum. If the car were accelerating away from you, you would say the car was orange in color, as the light would be shifting towards the red spectrum. We can conclude that knowledge is only Explicit in its given context. Context is therefore critical to the certification of Explicit knowledge.

Management of Explicit knowledge offers the most immediate impact for commercial organizations. Explicit knowledge is usually internal to an organization and is easily collected and assimilated into storage and delivery systems. Explicit knowledge is usually referred to as transactional, process or contextual information. Our objective with Explicit knowledge is to capture this information into technology to provide rapid and easy access to known facts.

"Collecting" is not the right term to describe our objectives for Tacit knowledge. In essence our objectives for Tacit knowledge management would, more or less, be the creation of a "knowledge map" that can point us quickly and efficiently to the repositories of relevant Tacit knowledge, which resides only in the minds of humans.

Plato also described knowledge in mathematical terms in order to demonstrate that knowledge is not based solely on the consensus of our five senses. Using a "point" as and example, a point is purely theoretical, as we cannot demonstrate a point with no dimensions and no start or finish. Since this concept is held in the human mind we refer to this knowledge as Tacit instead of Explicit.

Does Explicit knowledge really just mean we have enough perceived evidence to convince someone else to remove doubt? If this is the case then anyone that can remove someone else's doubt about something has created a fact in that specific context, but not necessarily the truth. Determination of the quality of knowledge is also a factor. In the absence of quality knowledge people will typically lean towards immediate or fast knowledge as opposed to performing the necessary research to find the best knowledge. This won't be the last time you read about this particular topic. Peoples preference for "fast" knowledge over "best" knowledge means that the location and ease of retrieval of quality knowledge is a significant aspect of a good knowledge management system.

Tacit knowledge is much more difficult to collect and assimilate as it typically requires an extrapolation of existing information and the input of interpolative information. Context becomes more ambiguous with tacit knowledge and therefore also introduces additional doubt.

Tacit knowledge is created in the minds of humans and therefore humans themselves have to become extensions of the KM systems we implement, as they are the only resource for tacit knowledge.

It's essential that the senior officers and the knowledge management team have a shared vision that incorporates the definition of Knowledge and the nature of the knowledge management mission. With the definition and mission statement providing the theory and organizational goals of KM then the delivery issues inherent to knowledge management do not revolve around the meaning of knowledge as much as what systems we need or desire to build to support the full Frid Decision-Cycle.

Gains Achieved by Implementing KM

Respondents from 423 cross-sectional organizations that have implemented a KM Program were asked to identify the benefits they have realized from KM:

The Survey Says!

71% - BETTER DECISION MAKING
68% - Faster response to key business issues
64% - Better customer handling

(KPMG Survey)

Now that's bang for your buck!

Ancillary Impact of Knowledge Management

Other than results shown in the survey above, what is another advantage of undertaking a Knowledge Management campaign?

The answer is *Change Creation.*

Let's ask ourselves, what is the one common denominator that all individuals interact with on a daily basis throughout an enterprise? The answer is knowledge. We require knowledge at every level of an organization to execute tasks and to grow as people.

In 1927 there was an experiment carried out at the Western Electric Company in Illinois by Elton Mayo. The experiment was called the Hawthorne experiment. Mayo hoped to discover optimum levels of plant illumination and proper timing of rest periods by experimenting with selected groups of workers. He discovered that it did not matter how the workers' environment was altered; merely being chosen for an experiment improved their productivity (the Hawthorne effect).

Mayo saw that the significant variable was not physiological but psychological. A series of experiments was performed, involving the assembly of telephone relays; test and control groups were subjected to changes in wages, rest periods, workweeks, temperature, humidity, and other factors. Output continued to increase no matter how physical conditions were varied; indeed, even when conditions were returned to what they had been before, productivity remained 25 percent above its original value. Mayo concluded that the reason for this lay in the attitudes of the workers toward their jobs and toward the company. Merely by asking their cooperation in the test, the investigators had stimulated a new attitude among the employees, who now felt themselves part of an important group whose help and advice were being sought by the company.

For this reason alone we can conclude that the sponsorship of knowledge management systems will involve everyone throughout the enterprise and will effect change. This change is psychological and will help to create a new attitude in the workplace. It's this change in attitude that will create an increase in productivity. Therefore we should strive to engage a long-term knowledge management campaign that reaches everyone in an organization and requires their input and certification of the knowledge data. The employees will react in a positive manor with a resultant increase in productivity.

So long as we provide positive change in any aspect of a workers daily life we should expect an increase in productivity. Knowledge management lends itself well to creating positive change, enterprise-wide.

If an organization is looking for primary gains in Performance then it needs to target the development of methodology, processes and systems to capture, present and analyze Explicit information.

If an organization is looking for primary gains in Innovation then it needs to target the development of methodology, processes and systems to stimulate, augment and broker Tacit knowledge. I cover knowledge brokering later on in the book.

What is a Knowledge Worker

How can we manage to "Not Manage"?

We have to either define or redefine our ideals about knowledge, but we also have to redefine our concept of management.

Let's start off with the management of knowledge workers. The bottom line is, you don't. When it comes to managing knowledge workers the best that we can hope to accomplish is to work with them to help develop their roles and responsibilities, manage their performance, manage their environment, manage the assignment of, and measure the quality of deliverables and provide mechanisms to manage the facilitation of innovation.

Our primary deliverable from knowledge workers is quality. If or when we achieve the level of quality output we require, only then can we begin to measure the quantity of output. Of course this means you need to be able to define what quality means to you, as it will mean something different to everyone. I have found that measuring quality is usually a judgmental process as opposed to an analytical process.

I have also found that putting a knowledge worker at the judgmental mercy of his or her piers is the most effective way of managing quality control. After all, knowledge workers are supposed to know more about their respective fields than their managers. This means that management will forever have difficulty assessing both performance and quality. Using piers as the control mechanism provides a reasonable level of confidence in measurement.

Pier group teams can be very powerful in the control of knowledge workers. By making pier-group teams accountable for specific deliverables and rewarding them as a team, this will usually provide rapid feedback if any one particular knowledge worker is inadequate.

A team of knowledge workers will often carry the burden of an inadequate team member for a short period of time but the inevitable conclusion is that the team will get tired of an individual not pulling their weight and take internal team corrective action. If internal team actions fail then the team will almost always request that management remove the defective knowledge worker. This makes management's job of quality and performance testing much easier. Management can then focus on what their primary mandate, which is: Results and Performance.

Words of warning though, don't send a knowledge worker into a team without carefully defining their roles and responsibilities or you are setting them and yourself up for failure. You also have to let the knowledge worker participate in the development of those roles and responsibilities as it defines the nature of their specialty, and who is better to decide on the nature of their roles and responsibilities other than knowledge workers themselves.

Their participation will also provide valuable feedback to better streamline their job, remove time-wasting obstacles and develop more efficient ways of achieving their deliverables. In other words they will apply classic business process engineering techniques to their own job function.

Knowledge Worker vs. Unskilled Labor

We no longer get to exercise the control and domination that management concepts have held so near and dear for so long over labor workers. Why not? Because there are fewer and fewer people involved in the manual labor process component of delivering a product or service. Therefore, those "control management" practices diminish in direct proportion to the diminishing manual laborers.

Manual laborers are being supplanted by modern day "knowledge workers". Knowledge workers don't lend themselves well to "control management" practices. So you may wonder where those unskilled laborers are disappearing too? Laborers aren't actually disappearing; they are being converted into knowledge workers.

The major industries of growth include medicine, education, technology, government and financial services. These growth industries have one distinct quality in common with each other; they require knowledge workers, not unskilled labor. That's one reason countries with large populations of unskilled labor such as China, Indonesia, Korea, etc. are having so much financial difficulty, and their difficulties will continue to escalate.

The demand for unskilled labor is decreasing while the demand for knowledge workers is increasing and will continue to increase. So the countries with a large population of unskilled labor are gaining an ever-increasing share of an ever-diminishing market. This is a clear sign of trouble.

The conversion of unskilled labor to knowledge worker has been most predominant in North America and Europe. Developing countries are struggling in this conversion primarily because they don't have the educational infrastructure that the United States and Canada has. Even Europe, for that matter, doesn't have the educational capacity of the US and Canada as their system of apprenticeship education is focused on the young and doesn't target the adult education markets.

The US and Canada's post secondary educational infrastructure will provide them a definitive advantage over the next twenty years as the working population increases in age, and the inevitable lack of younger workers will require the re-education and retention of older workers.

The inevitable lack of younger workers is caused by the decreasing birthrate in developed countries. In order to sustain the population of a given country you must sustain a birth rate of 2.1 births per woman (excluding children and seniors). Europe is running about 1.2 with some European countries running below 1.0, Japan runs close to 1.0 and North America is now approx 1.4. Each of the developed country's birth rates is still on the decrease. In contrast India's birth rate is approx. 2.5, Pakistan is 3.2, Saudi Arabia at 3.8, Malaysia is 2.5 and Mexico at 2.8 (based on the Central Intelligence Agency's 2001 statistics).

This means if all the declining countries started having baby's in order to catch up, it would still be about 20 years before these babies would enter the work force and probably another five years after that before they would be of any impact. But everybody is *not* having babies so it is guaranteed that we will be faced with a diminishing younger work force and will have no choice but to attempt to retain and retrain our older work force and/or increase the quota of legal immigrants.

The US and Canada have sufficient educational infrastructure and immigration policies to handle this requirement but other developed countries do not. This will also give the US and Canada a global advantage over the next 20-25 years at least.

Individual Characteristics of a Knowledge Worker

Let's step back in time to the time when you and I, and the ape shared a common ancestor. Anthropologists classify us in the category of "Hunter-Gatherers". Humans and apes have the biological and social infrastructure that creates for us a loose association and community. Knowledge workers get together when the need arises and disband when we have no further requirement to collaborate. This goes for socializing as well as productive work.

Knowledge workers are Hunter-Gatherers and will typically bind their loyalties to one person, mission or belief until they either lose faith or it no longer suits their needs. Then they move on to something more promising, based on the context of the moment.

Knowledge workers are not typically motivated by money, except for the fact that they demand to get paid very well for what they know. Adding a lot more cash to the offer makes them smile more but doesn't increase their enthusiasm to the project all that much. On the other hand, if they think you are not paying enough the effects are quick and dramatic. The scale doesn't work linearly in each direction unfortunately.

Knowledge workers are almost totally consumed by challenge and pier respect. They are ships of knowledge adrift on a sea of buyers, and periodically dock on someone's island long enough to trade knowledge for money, respect and most importantly, adventure.

So there it is in a nutshell. You don't manage knowledge workers, you provide them with awesome challenges and opportunities, spend your time broadcasting how great they are so they become more marketable for the next project, wherever that may be, and pay them handsomely for the fruits they bear, not on the amount of hours they work.

There is no sense asking the question "What do WE want?". They honestly don't care what you want. You need to be asking, "What do they want?" and build the environment to attract and keep them there as long as you can.

You can't really control knowledge workers, but you *can* control the environment they work in and turn them loose in it to produce results. That's what you really want after all, the end result. Why do you care how the bridge got built so long as it's exactly what the customer wants, it's the best bridge in the world, at the best price, delivered on time, and hopefully documented and reproducible after the knowledge workers have gone on to bigger and better challenges.

The fact is that knowledge workers have the upper hand today and will continue to do so for the foreseeable future. They don't need any one particular organization because they carry their own products in their head. The organization is the buyer, not the knowledge worker. Knowledge workers will never be employees in the classical sense, as they don't feel their survival depends on the survival of the organization or on anyone that works there.

Knowledge workers are assets, not liabilities. In current cost accounting systems, all employees are deemed liabilities, as they are a cost of sales or overhead. Accounting practices list buildings and equipment as assets though. But you have to ask yourself, what exactly does a building produce that adds value to the product or service for a customer. A building is an asset yet the salesman who sold the product and brought in the profits is a liability. As you can see, traditional accounting will need to change or at least offer multi-perspective views of the organization so we see the picture from a wealth creating perspective instead of a minimalist perspective.

Knowledge workers want and need to know they are assets. Management must see them as assets. Accounting systems must see them as assets. We list our assets and liabilities in traditional accounting systems so we can assess the value of a company in the event it is to be liquidated. We don't build companies with a business plan that states our sole intention is to liquidate this company. Who would ever invest in that?

We build business plans that demonstrate systems for achieving wealth. The primary way to accomplish this in the foreseeable future is through the effective application and management of knowledge worker culture. Therefore knowledge workers become the largest asset in the company.

So our objective for today and tomorrow's management is to cultivate and capitalize on both knowledge workers and knowledge management infrastructure.

Teams

Let's start at the top. There are three classifications of organizational structure: The Team, The Department and The Organization.

The Team is found throughout society. A team will consist of two to six members and will be bound by a loose association that targets a specific task or function. As I spoke of earlier, team members are hunter-gatherers and come together to perform a specific task or function then disband. Teams are usually formed quickly and causally and have no formal structure. No one is typically the "boss" although there is usually someone on the team that emerges as an untitled leader and guides the decision making process as the work progresses.

Within a team the unspoken role of team leader will often pass from one person to another depending on what function is being performed at that moment, dictated by the individual skill-sets required at that time. Teams are typically a democracy and everyone has a voice. Team interactions are usually passionate and intense as each team member relies on the others for a successful outcome, and success and failure to achieve the end result is obvious and immediate.

The Department usually consists of several teams. Studies have shown that departments are best kept to six teams or less. Departments often have a "boss" but the boss will usually proclaim that his or her group is really a democracy to avoid any contention that he or she is the dominant authority.

Regardless of declared democracy, someone in the department, whether it's the formally designated boss or not, will assume a leadership role to facilitate decision-making. This leader usually rises to the top because of other departmental members respect for their knowledge or organizational skills.

Whoever takes the leadership role will not typically lead by enforcing a dominant position, instead he or she will lead by example and attempt to achieve consensus amongst the departmental members. Departmental members are also usually well informed of everything that is going on and may offer input as they wish.

There are strong personal feelings of each departmental member to achieve the department's objectives as a whole and to work as synchronized unit. If a department grows to more than six teams then it usually destabilizes and fractionalizes into two separate departments. Too large a social and political structure cannot be maintained through consensus.

The Organization is a formal political mechanism to manage multiple departments. It does not operate on the same basis as Teams or Departments. There must be a formal line of authority as it is almost impossible to get everyone to agree on every issue.

Therefore someone or some group of people need to make decisions that will not please everyone all the time. Those that are displeased with decisions that have been made must conform to the top-level vote or leave the organization. The formal hierarchy also produces the necessary infrastructure for communications with other organizations. The organization provides the politics and bureaucracy for formal exchange outside the organization.

Size Counts

Team Size counts. Throughout the years I have worked on teams of various sizes, some more effective than others. The larger teams always seemed less productive and much more difficult to control than smaller teams. I started to muse that there must be some rationale that could be found that would tell me what the optimum team size should be and why.

During my research efforts I stumbled upon a book written by Collin Renfrew called "Theory and Explanation of Archaeology" that talks in depth about organizational structure and scalar stress. I can summarize the relevant sections quickly by stating, *"The ability to make decisions degrades rapidly as the team size grows beyond six."* Many studies have been made on the limitations of the human mind to determine capacities and limitations. The end result is that it appears the human mind only has the ability to handle up to seven concurrent functions simultaneously.

One such study by AT&T drew the same conclusions and became the basis for the eventual adoption of the seven-digit telephone number, with the rationale that the human mind could store and recall up to seven digits as a single unit of work. Additional numbers became more difficult to manage, as they didn't fit into the single memory chunks and needed to utilize two separate memory actions to recall the entire number.

After my research I looked back over time at my own experiences and found the similarities in previous teams I've worked on. Perhaps not the most objective review, but the results seemed very similar to my research findings. When working on a team of six or less people we always assumed a team approach with all of us carrying the same levels of responsibility and authority (no matter what the business card titles read). If another team member was added, someone almost always evolved subconsciously to become the team lead and we would always filter our project reporting back though this individual.

We didn't always formally declare a leader but someone would always assume this responsibility and we would all subliminally acknowledge the role. If we added more than six members to the team I could begin sensing the political edge that would begin shortly after the new member had acclimatized. The atmosphere would begin to tense in formal meetings and if the team had grown to eight members then even number made it difficult to break a tie when decisions were split. It became easier to break the project into two working teams that would report to a formal project manager. So in essence we demanded the nomination of a leader just to offload the politics that had begun to grow.

Nowadays I build all my teams with six or less people. Then I set out to prove that I am worthy of being a team member through demonstration of personal knowledge, compassion and vision. I work very hard to initially establish my credibility with the team because I find people put little stake in titles when working in a team environment. Team leaders will usually surface early because of the level of trust they gain by example.

A Brief History of KM

KM Timeline – 1980's

GENERATION 1

Technology is Everything

KM defined by "Data Warehousing" and stylized by the phrase "The right information in the right place at the right time". Technology was the "Answer".

KM Timeline – 1990's

GENERATION 2

Tacit vs. Explicit Information

"People" were finally recognized and introduced into the KM equation along with their "knowledge assets". It was eventually realized in late 1990's that not all knowledge assets could be made "Explicit".
Collaboration technologies were introduced.

KM Timeline – 2000's

GENERATION 3

Broken into three categories:

1. Content Management (What we Write)
2. Narrative Management (What we Say)
3. Context Management (What we Know)

(Snowden – IBM Institute of Knowledge Management)

KM – Content Management (What we Write)

- Categorization and Classification of :
  - Paper Assets
  - Digital Assets
- Taxonomies
- Meta-Data
- Relevancy Ranking
- Search
- Linguistic Relationships
- Valuation

(Snowden – IBM Institute of Knowledge Management)

KM – Narrative Management (What we Say)

The delivery of:

- **Face-to-Face (F2F) synchronous environments like:**
  Classrooms   **Conferences**
  Mentorship   **Small work groups**
  Trade Shows   **Meetings**
  Communities of practice in F2F environments

- **Virtual synchronous environments such as:**
  Teleconferences   Conference Software

- **Virtual asynchronous environments using**
  Collaboration Software.
  (Snowden – IBM Institute of Knowledge Management)

KM – Context Management (What we Know)

•Knowledge Brokering

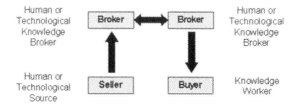

- **Experience Patterns**
- **Links to People and Information**

(Dr. Randy Frid)

Chapter 2–The Frid Decision Cycle

At the heart of every KM initiative you find the Frid Decision-Cycle. If you are to understand anything about knowledge management than this is it.

I must make an extremely important point at this juncture:

The human mind is only capable of performing two tasks:
Pattern Recognition and Response

From prenatal to early childhood the human brain is making and breaking synaptic connections in response to sensory input. With each repetition the connections between synapses strengthens until becoming permanent. In the early stages of development, if a particular sensory input illustrates a single condition, synapses may join temporarily in response to formulate a simple pattern. If the condition is not repeated then the synapses will break and be used within another pattern based on some other input. If the condition is repeated in a given timeframe the synaptic connections are further strengthened. With repetition the connections will become permanent, "hard wiring" the brain much like today's computer hardware.

Between ages 3–6 the synapses have finished hardwiring and we have developed a system for performing pattern recognition. From this point onward we will develop patterns based on soft connections (software) that allow us to manipulate our hardwired templates in a virtual fashion (similar to logic gates) and perform calculations to render "virtual" patterns and store them for future use as virtual connections between primary templates.

This is the primary reason why early education, exposure to parental, cultural and environmental sensory input hardwires our children with certain dispositions. Compensation patterns for deficiencies introduced during this process must be overcome in later years using virtual patterns, which are much harder to create and manage.

It's these patterns that allow us to negotiate through trillions of bits of parallel information and recognize components that don't match the pattern (such as the nickel that catches your eye, laying in the ditch when you're walking down the street). Our brains would be totally overwhelmed if we did not have some way of providing a preliminary filtration system. Every time our temperature rises we match a pattern and make adjustments to other bodily subsystems (condition/response). Every time we speak we assemble the sounds and match them to pre-developed patterns to understand the intent of the speech.

The list seems endless, and it is because the list seems endless that it becomes obvious that, with limited gray matter to work with, we must have a way to re-use patterns in multiple instances, each instance maintaining its own state information, and that the relationship between these patterns must be adjusted for context and relative value. Without such a system our mind would super-saturate in no time at all.

Experience derives from stored patterns. Intuition is simply the recognition of new relationships between patterns. You may feel that patterns can be of any size and complexity but if you look at the problems this raises you can see there must be "form and structure" to our analysis or we would become overwhelmed just managing the pattern generation system itself as a separate process altogether. A structured system also provides for optimum throughput although it also automatically implies boundaries to our capabilities.

All of this leads us to draw certain conclusions:

1. There must be a system behind pattern generation
2. The system must be finite to be manageable
3. The relationships between patterns must be analog to allow weighting
4. The system must employ re-entrant algorithms to facilitate evolution
5. The system must enable storage of multiple state information

With these constraints in mind I have formulated what I humbly call the "Frid Decision Cycle".

The Frid Decision-Cycle Defined:

Stage 1-Presentation of problem
Stage 2-Test personal experience
Stage 3-Gather information
Stage 4-Analyze information
Stage 5-Collaborate with experience
Stage 6-Draw conclusions
Stage 7-Execute
Stage 8-Test for success/failure
Stage 9-Apply success/failure feedback loop
Stage 10-Evolve

This Frid Decision-Cycle is possibly the *singularly most important concept to grasp* in knowledge management. It lies at the heart of what knowledge management is all about. We will explore this throughout the book.

The Frid Decision-Cycle

What problem do I need to solve?

⬤ = **What We Know**

▬ = **Relationship**

1. **Presentation of problem**
2. Test personal experience
3. Gather information
4. Analyze information
5. Collaborate with experience
6. Draw conclusions
7. Execute
8. Test for success/failure
9. Apply success/failure feedback loop
10. Evolve

What do I already know and can I draw conclusions based on that?

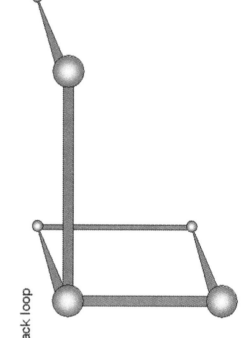

= **What We Know**

= **Relationship**

Do I have enough confidence to build yet?

1. Presentation of problem
2. **Test personal experience**
3. Gather information
4. Analyze information
5. Collaborate with experience
6. Draw conclusions
7. Execute
8. Test for success/failure
9. Apply success/failure feedback loop
10. Evolve

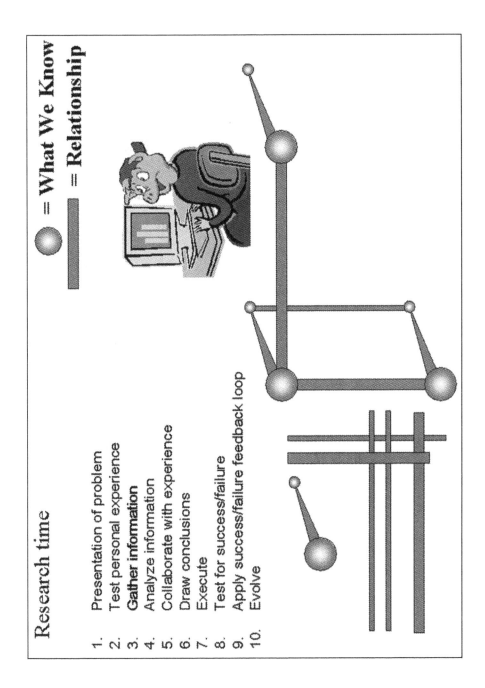

Figure out what is relevant to this situation

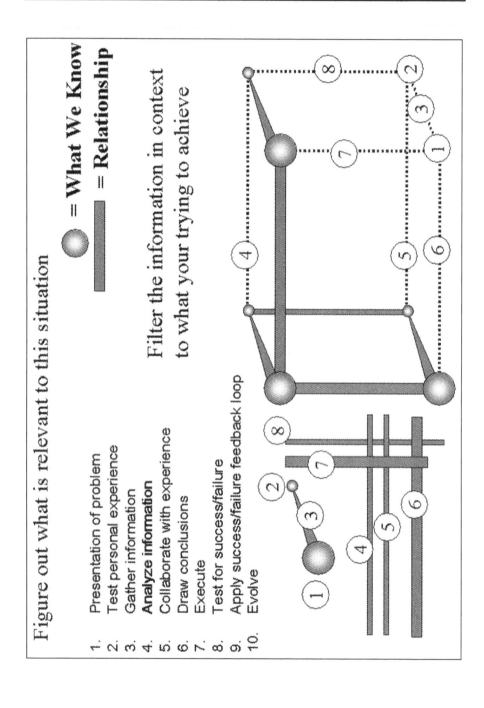

= **What We Know**

= **Relationship**

1. Presentation of problem
2. Test personal experience
3. Gather information
4. **Analyze information**
5. Collaborate with experience
6. Draw conclusions
7. Execute
8. Test for success/failure
9. Apply success/failure feedback loop
10. Evolve

Filter the information in context to what your trying to achieve

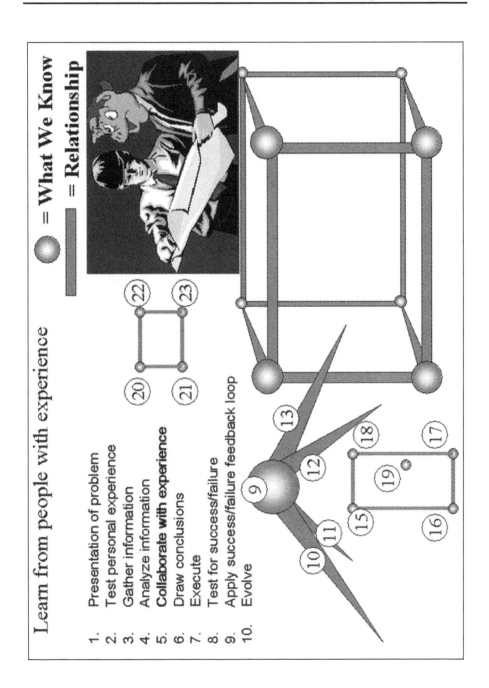

Learn from people with experience

= What We Know

= Relationship

1. Presentation of problem
2. Test personal experience
3. Gather information
4. Analyze information
5. **Collaborate with experience**
6. Draw conclusions
7. Execute
8. Test for success/failure
9. Apply success/failure feedback loop
10. Evolve

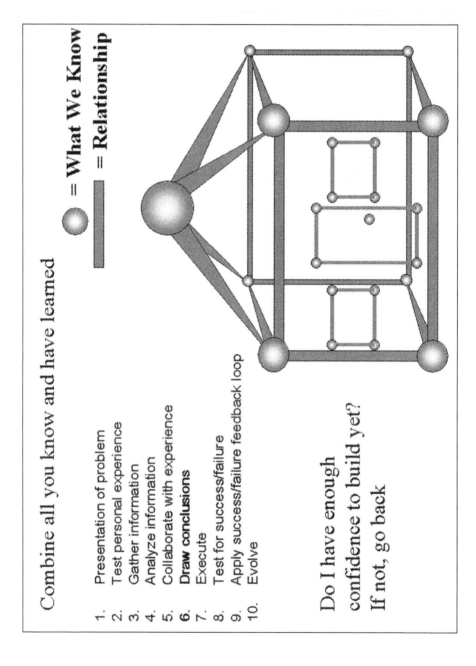

Combine all you know and have learned

● = **What We Know**

▮ = **Relationship**

1. Presentation of problem
2. Test personal experience
3. Gather information
4. Analyze information
5. Collaborate with experience
6. **Draw conclusions**
7. Execute
8. Test for success/failure
9. Apply success/failure feedback loop
10. Evolve

Do I have enough
confidence to build yet?
If not, go back

Give it a try

1. Presentation of problem
2. Test personal experience
3. Gather information
4. Analyze information
5. Collaborate with experience
6. **Draw conclusions**
7. **Execute**
8. Test for success/failure
9. Apply success/failure feedback loop
10. Evolve

Did it work?

1. Presentation of problem
2. Test personal experience
3. Gather information
4. Analyze information
5. Collaborate with experience
6. **Draw conclusions**
7. Execute
8. **Test for success/failure**
9. Apply success/failure feedback loop
10. Evolve

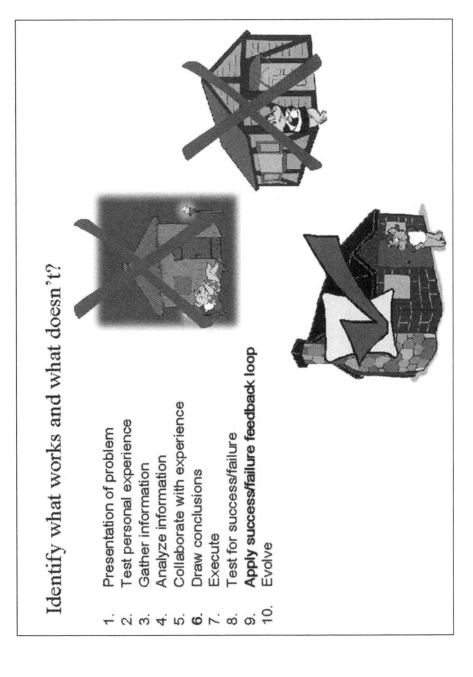

Identify what works and what doesn't?

1. Presentation of problem
2. Test personal experience
3. Gather information
4. Analyze information
5. Collaborate with experience
6. Draw conclusions
7. Execute
8. Test for success/failure
9. **Apply success/failure feedback loop**
10. Evolve

Learn from the experience and change the way we think?

1. Presentation of problem
2. Test personal experience
3. Gather information
4. Analyze information
5. Collaborate with experience
6. **Draw conclusions**
7. Execute
8. Test for success/failure
9. Apply success/failure feedback loop
10. **Evolve**

Chapter 3–KM verses IM

What is IM?

There is always confusion around the difference between **Information** Management (IM) and **Knowledge** Management (KM). These two functions are distinctly different yet inexorably interdependent. Perhaps the best method of describing their relationship is graphically.

Let's use a metaphor that describes the choices we make in Information Management as being akin to navigating a ship. You must first know which way you are heading at the moment, then, determine where you want to go, and finally, change your bearing. The same applies in technology. We figure out what problem we are trying to solve, choose an appropriate technology and then implement it. In the following illustration we can see "IM" two-dimensional navigation:

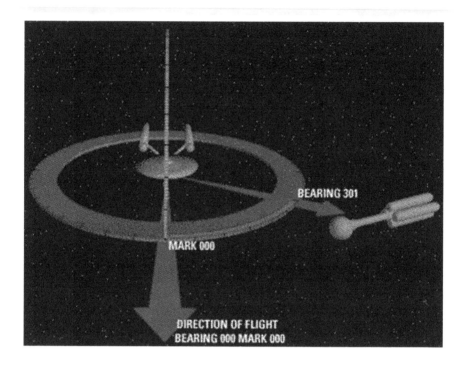

Being a technology ship on a flat corporate sea worked nicely in the old days of IT. Computer technicians and programmers were locked in a glass room with a big mainframe and never had to come out. You only had to tell them which direction to go and keep bringing them bigger and faster computer parts.

But that doesn't work any more. We eventually needed to reach beyond the surface of our planet and head for the skies and the vast reaches beyond if we were to grow. But in order to do this we needed to include an entirely new dimension.

When we talk about Knowledge Management we are really talking about a "new dimension" in our organizations. Our navigation systems (management strategies) must take into consideration this extra dimension if we are ever to go beyond our existing boundaries.

Look at the following illustration of "KM/IM" three-dimensional travel:

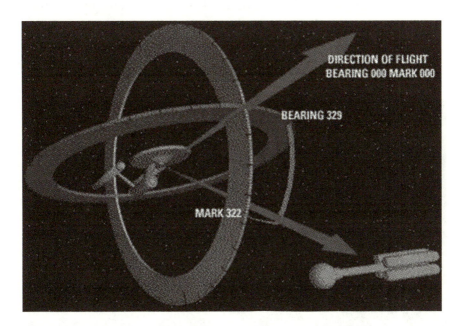

You can see buy the previous illustration that navigating in multi-dimensional space really requires the cooperation of two coordinate systems (and a third when you include time). It is true that IM and KM are different things, but without the integration of the two, neither really solves today's organizational navigation problems.

The old days of computer isolation have all but vanished. Nowadays, there is virtually no process implemented in an organization that does not have an integrated IT component. The IT itself influences the way we think about business processes, often just as much, and sometimes less or sometimes more, than the human component.

As you can see in this next illustration, Information Management tends to focus on explicit knowledge whereas Knowledge Management tends to focus on tacit knowledge and culture. The utilization of both dimensions allows us to properly re-align our organizations with much greater maneuverability to address change in any corporate direction.

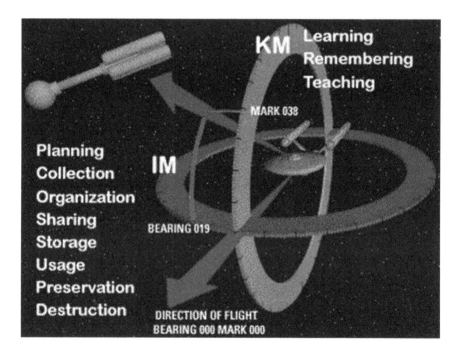

In today's organizations the CIO finds he or she must be both master and servant of two worlds: the business and the technology. The CIO must now extend outwards and incorporate an IT representative in the creation of every business process (the downfall is that most IT people are more comfortable with chips and logic then politics and organizational psychology). At the best of times the business folk think of technical people as propeller heads and the technical people tolerate these "users" while silently grinding their teeth. But the two cultures must blend, as, in the end, there is no choice in the matter.

With the blending of cultures we can recognize that there are both problems and opportunities. The problems can be annoying but the opportunities are great (more than the sum of their parts, if that is possible).

And so we have come to formalize and recognize this extra dimensional aspect of navigation and call it "Knowledge Management". With the integration of KM into the overall navigation system we are now capable of navigating in multiple dimensions.

Navigating three-dimensional space expands our capabilities as humans (exploration beyond the earth and beyond boundaries) and as organizations (expanding our knowledge, our awareness and our innovation).

With the recognition of KM in a multi-dimensional navigation equation we are required to now choose both a KM "*Mark*" and an IM "*Bearing*" to determine our true organizational direction. Once that new course is plotted we can move our organizations forward on the new integrated path.

This new integrated organizational path demands the recognition of both the human *Decision-Cycle* and the technological *Life-Cycle*.

Another way of putting it would be that:

KM manages the "Logical" (The Message)
- KM ensures people are asking the right questions

- KM helps people find "relevant" information
- KM helps people find subject matter experts (SME)
- KM helps broker the deal between buyers and sellers of information
- KM helps define relationships between information
- KM helps provide valuation of information

IM manages the "Physical" (The Messenger)

- IM provides tools to assist an information transaction
- IM provides the mechanics for binding Meta-Data to Data for context

(Data + Meta Data = Information)

I won't delve into IM philosophy, as that is not the focus of this book. But it is important to understand the relationship between IM and KM because they are inseparable. From this point forward I will only speak of IM in terms of how it is utilized in the implementation of KM programs.

KM & IM within the Decision-Cycle

Probably the best way for me to explain the individual responsibilities of IM and KM within the Frid Decision-Cycle is to build a table outlining our thought processes throughout a Frid Decision-Cycle and show the associated IM support processes and technologies beside it.

Human Deliverables

Before diving into the associated technologies that support KM initiatives it is good to remember that not all KM Programs need to be implemented using technology. Along with the technological deliverables we also need to support our KM efforts utilizing service deliverables such as:

➤ HR
➤ Teaching
➤ Presentations / Conferences
➤ Trade Shows
➤ Communications
➤ Workflow Integration
➤ Social Programs
➤ Mentorship Programs
➤ Workgroups / Meetings
➤ Physical Communities of Practice

These are ways for people to get together with people one-on-one or in a group and exchange information and ideas.

As for the technological side of the equation, please review the following table to get a better idea of where technology plays its part.

Frid Decision-Cycle Stage	How We Think	Supporting IM Processes	Technologies
1. Presentation of problem	Identify the problem Place in Context Prioritize Assess possible impact	Package the problem Deliver Package Ensure Delivery Feedback Success/Fail	Desktop Productivity Tools, Presentations, Conferences, Meetings, Hard Copy, E-Mail

2. Test personal experience	Input problem
	Identify similar experience patterns
	Identify gaps
	Attempt drawing a conclusion
	Determine confidence in conclusion
		If (KM confidence = High) {
		  Goto Step 7 "Execute"
		  (This is Conditioned Response)
		} Else { This step not applicable }
			Not Applicable

3. Gather information	Identify relevant questions Identify Categories and Classifications of Gap information Identify where to go to find Gap information	Present question relationship matrix Provide methods of Categorizing and Provide tools to help find information Broker information transactions	Question Matrix, Best Practices Search Engines, Databases, Web & File
4. Analyze information	Assess Content of information Assess Context of information Extend existing experience patterns Attempt drawing a conclusion Determine confidence in conclusion	Filter information Consolidate information Rank relevancy Identify related information Extrapolate information (what if's)	Data Warehousing, Artificial Intelligence, ERP Systems, HR & Accounting Systems
6. Collaborate with experience	Identify Subject Matter Experts (SME) Engage SME's or Brokers Relay Contextual Problem Input feedback and extend patterns Attempt drawing a conclusion Determine confidence in conclusion	Identify Subject Matter Experts (SME) Notify SME's Connect with SME's Broker the deal with SME's	Groupware, Communities of Practice, SME Software, Tele/Video Conferencing, On-Line Mentorship Programs (broadcasts), On-Line Meetings (Messenger), On-Line Socials/Chat (forums)

Frid Decision-Cycle Stage	How We Think	Supporting IM Processes	Technologies
6. Draw conclusions	Adjust weights between information relationships for Choose best-fit pattern + extension Draw final conclusion Determine confidence in conclusion	Artificial Intelligence	Neural Networks
7. Execute	Identify recipients for solution Structure communications Communicate solution	Locate recipients Identify how recipients can receive Package solution Broker the communications Ensure delivery	Presentations, Meetings, Hard Copy, E-Mail
8. Test for success/failure	Monitor impact of solution Perform Actual vs. Projected Weight impact of all factors Determine confidence in assessment	Measure output of solution in relation to Perform comparative analysis Generate reports Deliver reports and ensure delivery	Performance Measurement, Benchmarking
9. Apply success/failure feedback loop	Add additional context from tests Adjust weights in pattern + extension Reinforce weights that proved correct Reduce weights that proved incorrect Consolidate final pattern + extension Create additional questions	Adjust brokering techniques Adjust delivery methods Adjust analysis calculations Adjust rules, thresholds and triggers Adjust information resources Adjust categories and classifications Adjust question matrix	Change Management Tools
10. Evolve	Adjust feedback algorithms (upgrade the change-management system)	Adjust feedback algorithms (upgrade the change-management)	Change the Change Management Tools

Chapter 4–The Knowledge Broker

Shortly after World War II, management began concentrating on pushing decision-making down in the enterprise. Why? This is a question for historians. Common belief is that the business of production of goods and the delivery of services began to implement higher levels of sophistication as a result of pioneering breakthroughs made in response to the war effort.

Today, when historians are asked why the alliance won the war, they respond in a manner very different to the response of our parent's generation. Historians tell us, quite simply, that allied countries out-manufactured the enemy. This superior level of production arrived through the application of scientific management principles developed in North America earlier in the century. With the advent of "scientific management" came the birth of the "knowledge worker" and the beginning of the end for the unskilled laborer. Did the unskilled laborer just disappear? No, they were forced to become educated as a simple matter of survival and because educational tools became more prevalent for the masses.

So as employees got smarter, this movement began placing bigger demands on management. Existing decision-making hierarchies traditionally focused on all decisions being made at the top levels of an organization. This methodology began to dilute for a couple of reasons.

The first reason is that it was taking too long to make smaller decisions. Both global and local competition was on the increase and becoming more intellectual.

The second reason was the growing realization by senior executives that they could begin partially delegating decision-making responsibilities to a growing base of skilled employees and achieve better and faster results while still maintaining their authority on critical issues. In fact, their capacity to react to change actually extended beyond what they could have controlled under traditional circumstances, by leveraging the additional capabilities in their growing intellectual worker-base. This was the beginning of a win-win situation for workers and management alike.

Because of the changes introduced by WWII, the decision-making process has been a major target of many re-engineering efforts. As part of these undertakings, organizations regularly create new organizational models to accommodate changes in economics, environment, culture, geography, trends and fads, as well as numerous other reasons. Some of these changes can be induced, controlled and managed, while others are purely reactive.

So, with the great organizational minds on the planet concerned about the delegation of decision-making, why have historical efforts been so very difficult for organizations to implement? The answer lies in the very nature of human thought.

Let's look at a classic organizational chart:

Classic Organizational Hierarchy:

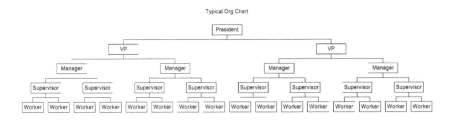

There is nothing unusual to be seen here. Actually this style of classic hierarchy is used in most commercial, government and military organizations today. Why do we use a structure like this? The reason is simple in that it allows units of work to be clustered in a logical fashion, isolated by task, product, service or any other method we see fit to approach the organization of processes and responsibilities.

So does it work? The answer is "partially", but limited in scope. The scope of this hierarchy is used to control the downward push of information, not upward pull. Commands originating from the top are designed to propagate down, gaining momentum and detail before reaching the bottom.

So is this not, in effect, a decision-support system? The answer is no, this is a command-support system.

In order to do a comparison between the two different types of systems we first need to understand the ten fundamental steps that each of us go through when making a decision (also referred to as The Frid Decision-Cycle as described in the chapter called The Frid Decision Cycle).

The Frid Decision-Cycle:

Stage 1-Presentation of problem
Stage 2-Test personal experience
Stage 3-Gather information
Stage 4-Analyze information
Stage 5-Collaborate with experience
Stage 6-Draw conclusions
Stage 7-Execute
Stage 8-Test for success/failure

Stage 9-Apply success/failure feedback loop
Stage 10-Evolve

You can see by the stages above that a command-based support system really only satisfies stage 1. Therefore, the fixed hierarchical approach is only a single component in the full Frid Decision-Cycle.

So why do we typically implement this type of organizational model and not a model more supportive of decision-making? We implement this model because it is simple to comprehend and provides a linear model of authority. This system does not accommodate iterative processing and feedback mechanisms required for decision-making. The hierarchy is primarily adopted because of its efficiency in propagating unidirectional orders and communications. This is efficient in classic military environments but breaks down completely in today's decentralized knowledge-worker cultures.

Because of the need for speed in decision implementation under battle conditions, military decision-making will often jump from Stage 2–"Test personal experience" directly to Stage 7–"Execute". This is referred to as "Conditioned Response". Therefore, commanders with a large breadth of personal experience are greatly valued in these circumstances. Inexperienced commanders equate to significantly increased risk in this scenario.

On the other hand, when the situation is not life or death (fight or flight) then both military and non-military organizations recognize greater benefits from the adoption of the full Frid Decision-Cycle. The rewards are greater because the full Frid Decision-Cycle mitigates risk.

The Frid Decision-Cycle itself is, quite simply, our physiological and psychological means of reducing risk thereby increasing our probability of success.

Because the full Frid Decision-Cycle is a broad topic and one that cannot be appreciably accommodated in a single book, I have chosen this section to focus on one aspect of the Frid Decision-Cycle that deals with the brokering of knowledge.

In Knowledge Brokering we have three principle players:

> Knowledge Buyer
> Knowledge Broker
> Knowledge Seller

The following diagram shows the three types of players in action. You can sense how informational requirements for decision-making can often extend beyond the boundaries of an organization:

Knowledge Brokering:

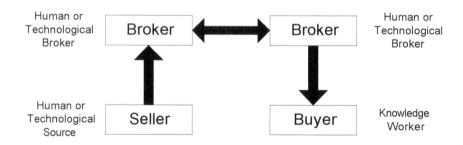

This trinity of functions can be a combination of both people and technology. These three entities are pooled to dynamically model and extend existing patterns of knowledge. If we ask ourselves what makes a "*senior*" executive, the answer would be "experience" (except on occasions when it's the bosses nephew or such). Typically experience is gained over time as an individual becomes exposed to larger quantities of problems, negotiates the answers (success and failures) and develops a substantial library of experience patterns to draw upon. This evolution is also obtained, in part, through the application of re-entrant algorithms (also known as feedback loops).

However, in the real world these human repositories of experience are not usually associated with management positions alone and are more often than not, found distributed throughout the workforce and/or external to an organization. I refer to these people as Subject Matter Experts (SME).

The typical management hierarchy in today's society is usually implemented in support of GAAP (Generally Accepted Accounting Principles) and as a line of authority. GAAP is linear with well-defined rules, thresholds and triggers. GAAP is for structured financial reporting.

Unlike the GAAP hierarchy, the human resources that form the framework of experience necessary for survival and innovation participate in a dynamic, hidden matrix both internal and external to the organization. The tendrils of decision-support will extend beyond the physical confines of a simple two-dimensional hierarchy. This knowledge lattice will work on multiple levels and in multiple dimensions.

The following diagram depicts the hidden universe of decision-making that underlies any formal structure:

The Hidden Decision Matrix:

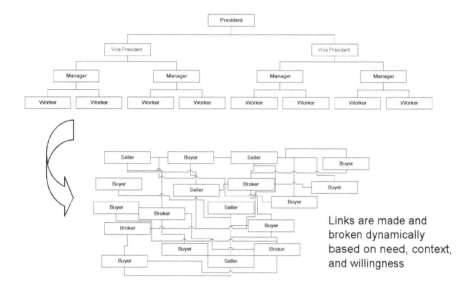

Links are made and broken dynamically based on need, context, and willingness

Go back and look again at *Classic Organizational Hierarchy* illustration and recognize its simple two-dimensional structure. Now think about the last time you ever saw anyone that was in the process of making a decision actually referencing the corporate org chart. The reference would only be made if the org chart itself were a component of the research requirements.

So what are Buyers, Brokers and Sellers? Just as you might think, Buyer's are people in need of knowledge. Brokers are people or systems that might not have the answer but know where to go to get it and may facilitate the transaction (librarians make an excellent example of a knowledge broker). Sellers are people or systems that contain the required knowledge that may or may not wish to sell.

You'll notice that I have now begun to speak of systems as well as people. The reason for this is because technology can play a large part in our knowledge management infrastructure because we can design our Frid Decision-Cycle support tools to handle dynamic linkages of information resources and subject matter experts as well as to cluster information in logical units applicable to circumstance and context.

When I speak of dynamic linkages I refer to the ability of using technology to input and extract information from multiple perspectives (dimensions) based on the context of the problem being addressed at this particular moment in time. This forces us to approach knowledge buying and selling from both known and conceptually related points of view. Technology can act as a knowledge broker by finding buyers and sellers and negotiating willingness, scope, cost, access privileges as well as other services required for the bartering of information.

Paramount in the concept of building a KM system that is capable of supporting the full Frid Decision-Cycle is the ability to capture the experiences and best practices of experienced people throughout different aspects of an organization. Technology can assist us by performing several tasks such as allowing knowledge workers to dynamically make and break new relationships with information systems and repositories as well as store lessons learned.

Part of a good KM system will also provide us the ability to allow knowledge workers to connect with each other dynamically (both synchronously and asynchronously) for alliances between individuals and groups as well as create "virtual teams" also referred to as "communities of practice" where people can benefit from the experiences of each other in related areas of interest or concern.

The technologies we decide to engage in support of the Frid Decision-Cycle should be designed from the outset to run independent of fixed management hierarchies and reporting structures. Yet, by closely assessing the activities within KM technologies management can see patterns of who communicates with whom, who contributes information (sellers), who is most frequently requesting information (buyers) and which people and systems mediate most frequently (brokers). Based on these measurements, management can make substantiated assessments as to how they can stimulate specific areas of knowledge brokering and encourage the growth of innovation in the enterprise.

Management can also define business rules, thresholds and triggers that can be incorporated into KM systems that can participate in the decision-making processes beneath the covers. In other words, a well-crafted KM system can be trained to absorb senior management experience and provide influence on the overall information made available and how decisions are formulated.

When building systems that support the Frid Decision-Cycle we must always take into account underlying human psychological requirements that influence the success or failure of any KM initiative.

An important "Rule of Thumb" in Knowledge Management:

"People prefer fast information over best information"

Knowing this at the outset, we can then recognize that a key goal of any knowledge management program is to find the most relevant information, filtered in context to the problem at hand, as fast as possible. This point cannot be stressed enough. Any KM system that is slow or complicated will quickly pass into oblivion once the novelty wears off.

So what does this mean to Knowledge Managers?

It means that we, as Knowledge Managers, should think in the following terms:

> Knowledge Management <u>Theory</u> is Strategic, but
> Knowledge Management <u>Implementation</u> must be tactical

In other words: ***To be Practical-it has to be Tactical***

With the lack of time people have for anything these days, coupled with the over-abundance of available information, people are trying to figure out where to best spend what little time and attention they have. This means that issues surrounding culture and technology are well and fine, but the bottom line is we need to deliver quantifiable implementations, and the product of those implementations, quickly. In order to do that, we need to fight and win small battles instead of trying to fight the entire war.

Deliver tangible results in a tightly focused environment, and the good word will spread. Each conquest will fuel the fire as well as open purse strings for financing further ventures. Each small win will raise confidence and provide an increasing knowledge of what works and what doesn't. Use the knowledge gained from tactical implementations to define and refine the overall strategy.

To summarize: ***KM <u>Strategy</u> is the leveraging of <u>Tactical</u> implementations***

So as we begin to think about tactical implementations as subsets of an overall KM strategy, then one place any organization can start is by developing tools that us help broker information.

One type of Knowledge Broker

If you analyze the way most people make decisions within their work environment you will typically find that most individuals will rely heavily on the immediate workgroup that surrounds them physically. Communication is typically informal, and mentoring (the transfer of information from one to another) flows freely, in most circumstances, because of trust. Trust is established almost subconsciously in physically situated teams because each person's actions influence each other's survivability. In these situations, we are our own knowledge-brokers and negotiate the transfer of knowledge based on our established levels of trust.

So is this where we should deploy a knowledge-broker system? Absolutely NOT! Why not? Because it is very difficult to improve on physical face-to-face communications and anything technologically introduced to foster additional interaction at this level will introduce time and complexity and will therefore be in conflict with the rule that people prefer fast information over best information.

So how would knowledge managers introduce a knowledge-broker system and its associated technologies into their organizational environment? One way is by implementing an enabler of cross-functional communications.

Lets look at a scenario where Group A is building interstellar rocket ships and Group B is building lunar golf carts. Different tasks but there are functional similarities at different levels based on roles.

Group A has project managers and so does Group B. Group A has mechanical engineers and so does Group B. So now we can implement a knowledge-broker known as "communities of practice": one for

Project Managers, another one for Engineers, and possibly one for each separate project. In these separate and individualized communities we will have such tools as discussion forums, shared best-practices databases, shared risk management systems, shared document repositories, shared contacts, shared links to internal and external resources, and shared question matrices (for a start).

Although each group may be on opposite sides of the world their respective virtual community fosters communications between individuals with similar interests and concerns. People typically choose their careers based on what they like to do, or what they are best at. It is safe to say that they are motivated to interact with others of the same background, interests or ambitions. As individuals, the participants in these communities strive to obtain similar goals as we as humans strive to achieve in communities outside the workplace: Respect, Recognition, Appreciation, Friendship, Help and a certain comfort in knowing we belong to something bigger than ourselves.

Knowing how similar interests foster social communities we can comfortably invest in this "low-hanging-fruit" and utilize technology to bring together people and their implied experiences over vast distances. The technology becomes, in this essence, the "Knowledge Broker", the Enabler.

There are lots of extra parts and pieces required, like sponsorship, advocacy, management and measurement when implementing a community of practice, but the recognition that a community of practice is just one form of "Knowledge Broker", and that all Knowledge Brokers exist for the sole purpose of supporting the Frid Decision-Cycle, will keep your sites focused on the underling principle of why a community will come into being and why it will eventually fail.

Knowledge Broker Summary

The Frid Decision-Cycle lies at the heart of everything we do. From deciding what TV show we'll watch tonight to deciding whether or not to open that new manufacturing plant in Detroit, the Frid Decision-Cycle is our human system of analysis.

Our KM processes and technologies must recognize and address this fundamental flow of information and knowledge processing. Our KM technologies must help broker information and human connections that are necessary to support the Frid Decision-Cycle.

Knowledge Management, in its purest form, is merely a servant of the Frid Decision-Cycle. A tool. A method of providing better connections to a greater repository of filtered and context-sensitive experience and information than has ever been available to mankind before the latter half of the 20th century.

The Knowledge Broker plays a significant and inseparable role in the full Frid Decision-Cycle and an understanding of this role is paramount in building lasting and beneficial KM programs.

Chapter 5-HELP

The Heuristic Enterprise Learning Program

The concept behind HELP (Heuristic Enterprise Learning Program) is founded in the roots of knowledge brokering. We discussed the premise that people typically have an intrinsic desire to place a value on their Tacit knowledge and as such treat it as a commodity. We experience this in our everyday lives when we need to know something. We approach another individual (the seller) who we hope can provide us with some insight on a particular subject matter. The seller listens to the request, evaluates the individual requesting the knowledge (the buyer) and begins the process of mentally assessing the value of the knowledge in relation to the relationship with the buyer.

Trust is extremely important in the barter process because trust formulates the basis for an easy and immediate exchange. If the seller has had good historical experiences dealing with the buyer then the seller knows that if he/she sells the knowledge that there is a high likelihood that the buyer will reciprocate one day when the seller is in need of knowledge. This is the fastest form of negotiation.

If the buyer is not personally known but has a reputation that has preceded him or her for participating in knowledge exchange then the price is a little higher and introduces a little hesitation, but the transaction will likely go through. The buyer will be put in a sort of credit situation until the seller has the chance to reciprocate and test the value of the credit. Often, key details may be withheld during the initial knowledge transaction and held in reserve until the credit can be put to the test. If the credit is OK during the reciprocating transaction then further transactions should allow the free flow of knowledge without reservation.

If the buyer is unknown to the seller, and has no preceding reputation, or has a reputation for assuming credit for others knowledge, then the response to the request may be varied and unpredictable. Some sellers may outright refuse to transact, others may politely inform the buyer they don't have the knowledge or the time, others may demand public credit before proceeding, others (usually outside the organization) will place a monetary value on the knowledge. Typically, inside and organization, the monetary value of knowledge is negotiated during the hiring process and is renegotiated incrementally as a salary increase or performance bonus. There are many ways to respond to distrust, and the higher the level of distrust the higher the price the seller sets on the commodity.

The reason a seller is willing to sell their product is also varied. Motivators are money, respect, notoriety, privilege, security, fear, etc...I don't feel we can isolate and develop systems for the myriad of reasons for sale. We can definitely build infrastructure to assist in the transactional process and help cultivate an environment where individuals can better assess and negotiate trust levels.

The final form of transaction is the knowledge broker that may not have the solution but may know of someone that does. This form of transaction is also dependent on trust level and the motivations for sale are also varied. This type of transaction is also an important part of a complete knowledge transfer system in organizations of any size.

HELP as a Knowledge Map and Accreditation System

Why do we what to build a HELP system? The answer is that the HELP system will build a *dynamic* enterprise knowledge map that identifies those individuals that are willing to participate in knowledge transfer as well as the areas in which they may offer Tacit knowledge on specific subjects.

So how can we develop a system using technology to facilitate knowledge transactions and trust negotiation?

The Heurist Enterprise Learning Program (HELP) is a one type of dynamic knowledge broker system.

The 10-step method is as follows:

1. The system sends out an e-mail daily to all staff
2. Daily response is mandatory as part of staff's base job description
3. The e-mail asks 6 questions:
    a. Did someone help you with a problem today?
    b. If so, who?
    c. Nature of the problem?
    d. Nature of the solution?
    e. Was the problem solved (completely, partially, not solved)?
    f. If "Not Solved" was the seller able to refer someone else?
4. The response is parsed and results stored in a database
5. The buyer is awarded 3 credits for completing the form

6. The seller is awarded 20 credits for Solved, 10 for partial, 5 for referral

7. A search front-end is built to access the database

8. Buyers search the HELP knowledgebase to identify potential sellers

9. Seller information is available on-line so they can be located and engaged

10. The database is regularly analyzed to determine whom the buyers and sellers are, what areas of expertise they offer, the frequency of each participant and the level of skill of individual sellers to resolve problems and transfer their Tacit knowledge. Frequent use by individual buyers can also help point to areas where specific buyers may need additional training or support.

The results of analyzing the knowledge base can then be used to develop recognition programs based on earned credits. Rewards can range from public recognition to monetary bonuses or promotion.

Developing an enterprise scale knowledge map is a ferociously complex task given that Tacit knowledge continues to grow with experience and changes in environment and job functionality. Maintenance of a manual system is time consuming, expensive and prone to high levels of inaccuracy. By automating the process of knowledge map development and binding it back to one or more reward programs works well with the concept that individuals place value on their knowledge and expect to sell their knowledge.

The two most relevant questions in the e-mail are: Who provided help and the nature of the problem. The rest of the information is useful for analysis but the first two really build the foundation for the knowledge map. These two questions identify who the sellers are, how willing they are to participate, and the areas they are knowledgeable in.

Of course, the message delivery and retrieval system can really be anything that serves the same functionality. If you would prefer to have a message pop up on the screen of a mainframe terminal that collects the same information then the results will be the same. It is really the intent as opposed to the delivery mechanism.

The HELP program is showing you one way of how we can utilize technologies in the Knowledge Broker methodology and encourage people to participate in systems with both rewards and recognition. The HELP program also demonstrates one way that management can use technological tools in assessing levels of participation and the identification of knowledge "silo's" that need to be harvested.

Most importantly, a HELP style system should be integrated into daily workflow for automated collection of this type of information. Integration into workflow is the ultimate goal so the process of KM becomes transparent to workers. If it is not integrated into the daily workflow people will just keep telling you that they simply "don't have time" to respond to additional emails during their busy workday. If you can capture the same information during order entry or work-order signoff, or some other normal duty then the process becomes somewhat invisible and there will be less "push-back".

Chapter 6–Taxonomies

"Taxonomies are <u>NOT</u> Directory structures"

There, I said it.

In the business context, taxonomy is best described as "The classification of information in an ordered system that indicates natural relationships."

Business taxonomies deal with information, not physical documents. Documents can reside anywhere. It doesn't really matter. We only really care about the stuff inside the documents.

And therein lies our problem.

The "stuff" inside the documents can be valuable information to someone. You may not think so, but they might. You also might consider that some of the information is not even related to other information but someone else might believe otherwise.

For instance, I might think that a "CLUB" is a place to go to get a drink, dance and have fun, and therefore classify it as such. You, on the other hand, might consider a "CLUB" something a caveman uses to hit something or someone with and classify it as such. Someone else may classify it as one of the four suits in a deck of playing cards. Yet another person thinks of a "CLUB" in terms of an object to connect to the steering wheel of your car so someone can't steal it.

Knowing that any one piece of information can relate to many different things leaves us with two main ways of categorizing it.

1. The manual classification method.

This method requires someone to review the content of the document and decide how to classify it and then tag it with the required categories that allow it to be found when a user searches.

Why is this good?

Manual tagging is good because it ensures a reasonable level of accuracy and ensures the document is at least bound to some relevant categories. For example, there is no need to relate the "CLUB" referred to in a document on golfing to the category called "Automobile Accessories". This is the method that companies such as "Yahoo" use at the moment.

Why is this bad?

Manual tagging is bad because it takes a lot of work and time and never guarantees that all related categories would be tagged to the document.

2. The automatic classification method

By using automated search tools to parse through the text of a document we can make note of the words in the document and test the words against predefined rules in an automated system and the system itself can then tag the document with categorical relationship tags.

Why is this good?

Automatic tagging is good because it vastly accelerates the time required to get large document repositories (corpus) indexed and categorized.

Why is this bad?

Automatic tagging needs rules to work by, which take significant time to create and adjust. Accuracy is always questionable and the importance of relationships between information is almost impossible to establish in advance.

So what will work?

First we need to grasp a bit better how the average person searches for information. Normally a person doesn't just enter just one word when searching (i.e.: "Club"). Normally a person will enter in multiple words that provide much better context (i.e.: "Golf Club" or "Night Club").

So in essence we aren't really dealing with words, we are dealing with phrases. This is an important concept to grasp. Most available search engines utilize "key word" search, but most of our requirements are "key phrase" search requirements.

Why doesn't every search engine use Key Phase searching?

Most search engines use Key Word search capabilities because it is easy and fast to implement. Key Phrase searching is complicated and requires a significant understanding of linguistics. It simply becomes too cost prohibitive for most vendors to invest that amount of time or energy developing a decent search tool.

There is also another need that is, for the most part, avoided by search engine designers: "Relationships"

In order to properly classify a piece of information we need to understand what other information it relates to. This is what evaluates the context of the information and makes sure it is bound to all of the related categories that it should be. This requirement also stipulates the need to understand, what is a strong relationship and what is a weak relationship.

There is a relationship between the Golf Club and the Caveman Club, albeit, fairly weak. That doesn't mean that one doesn't exist. What if someone was doing research on "clubs used as tools" in the evolution of man? Both would fit and would probably find a natural evolution pattern.

So what is all this leading up to?

In a nutshell, when we build taxonomies we need to:

1. Separate our thinking from the existing document structure of the organization and only think "information".

2. Build our categories based on the natural order of how information is grouped logically for our specific industry.

3. Develop our preliminary skeleton taxonomy. As a best practice I would not advise creating more than three levels of depth to your tree. Two levels are preferred. Use more taxonomies (dimensions) instead of deeper levels.

4. Use automated tools to parse our document repositories to extract a lexicon of phrases instead of words and count the number of occurrences of each phrase for ranking. Ranking can also be a controversial issue because counting phrases or words in a specific document does not necessarily mean the information is more valuable, just more often repeated. It should be recognized at this point that a corpus containing documents of significantly varying

size would produce ambiguous ranking results. Compensation algorithms can be written but are very interpolative.

5. Latch the phrases to the relevant categories in the taxonomy (manually or automatically).

6. While searching documents for phrases we should also be extracting phrases that co-occur in the same body of information (i.e.: Golf Club, Flexible Graphite) and count how many times each co-occurrence happens in the same body of information so we get an idea of relevance of the relationship.

7. Search for relationships between disparate bodies of similar information (similar or related information in different documents), count these occurrences and co-occurrences as well and derive relevancy and ranking across documents (conceptually related relationships).

8. Bind all of the above results to the taxonomy and refine the taxonomy by performing "spot checks" on random documents to ensure they show up under the categories you want them to. If they don't, then you will need to extract additional phrases or ensure that phrases previously extracted are properly bound (latched) to the categories you want them to. This is an on-going process.

9. Create additional taxonomies based on alternate logical methods of grouping the same information. Each taxonomy should satisfy a different business requirement. Use the existing phrases you

extracted into lexicons in step 4 and latch them to your additional taxonomies. Refine the taxonomies.

10. Produce a user-friendly (point and click) taxonomy navigation system that users can utilize without the user having to drill down 20 layers in the taxonomy before they get close to what they need. Do this by building a multiple-taxonomy navigation interface that allows users to make multiple sections from multiple trees. The selections would aggregate to become a combined search filter.

Using the taxonomy for "Finding"

There is a strategic advantage to creating multiple logical taxonomies bound to the same corpus.

If the multiple taxonomies are made available at the time a user begins a search, you can present them the option of making multiple choices within and across multiple taxonomies to narrow their scope of search.

Picture that one taxonomy could be based on a geographical hierarchy, another on products or services, and yet one more taxonomy based on department.

With three or four different taxonomy hierarchies present the user could open each one and select different nodes from the taxonomy tree that will narrow their search dramatically. The user could make choices as to whether or not each taxonomy node's context must appear in the search results before any documents should be returned. This can be designed in Boolean fashion, using AND/OR/NOT relationships.

This principle allows the user to basically return only information that intersects in multiple dimensions.

What is really happening is that we are adding and removing complete contexts to and from our search parameters instead of just adding and removing keywords. Per the illustration below, if the user selected the "Golf" category from the "Products" taxonomy, they would actually be adding "Products", "Sporting Goods", and "Golf" to the context search. By turning on and off different nodes in the different taxonomies, the user is viewing the same corpus of data from different viewpoints (or dimensions). Turning off "Golf" would then force the removal of any references to "Products" if there were no other selections made within the "Products" taxonomy tree.

Based on a search for "Club" we could further localize our results by adding additional filtering dimensions from the taxonomy as the following graph illustrates:

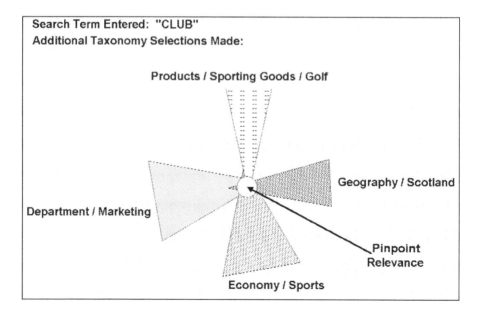

Your taxonomies can therefore be used to pre-filter information using a simple point-and-click methodology that is bound directly to your investment in categorizing your organizations digital assets. This both simplifies and enhances usability of the organization taxonomy.

This taxonomy-based filter is very powerful and greatly increases the relevancy of your results by orders-of-magnitude.

Utilizing three or four taxonomies in search filtering reduces your returned "hits" exponentially, both enhancing and serving our rule that "people prefer fast information over best information" while still providing greater relevancy. There is nothing worse than your search engine telling you it has found 1000 documents that match your criteria. Nobody is going to search through 1000 documents, even if it's the 932nd document that is the most relevant.

By utilizing several taxonomies we can also keep our taxonomy depth quite shallow. We don't want to make it difficult for users to find what they're looking for by having to drill down many levels in a taxonomy tree. They'll get frustrated quickly and drop or circumvent the system.

You will want to keep your taxonomy depth less than three levels and preferably only two levels.

Breaking your taxonomy navigation into multiple, shallow taxonomies will allow the users to filter by simple logical segregation instead of having to understand, in advance, how someone or some software decided to categorize any particular piece of information.

The aggregation of selections made across multiple taxonomies provides the same level of filtration but in a very user-friendly way.

It is important to recognize that this system of taxonomy filtration can be applied across many IT systems simultaneously (such as in a portal environment). In this way, a user could have several portal objects opened in the same browser window (i.e.; ERP system, sales order system, contacts, emails, documents, discussions, etc.) and all of the objects could simultaneously filter their context to provide only information that matches the criteria defined by the taxonomy selections. This provides a very powerful way to dimension multiple systems and views into information.

Note: There is also a law of diminishing returns if you implement too many taxonomy selections within a single search.

Sample Taxonomy Display

You can see in the next illustration that the user has chosen to find relevant documents by only choosing two top-level categories from two different taxonomies. No additional search criteria should be required although they could always add key words to their search or continue making selections of additional categories or subcategories for further filtration (which could also be called Dimensioning the Information).

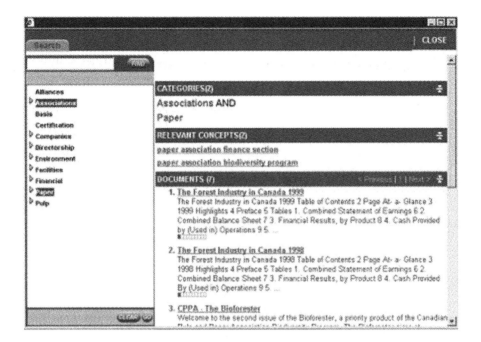

You can see under the CATEGORIES heading that the user has also chosen to use the Boolean "AND" operation across multiple taxonomies. Any additional selections would aggregate in this display so the user would always have a visual representation of what dimensions they have added to the search criteria. Booleans should also work within a single taxonomy.

The following illustration demonstrates the use of Boolean "OR" functionality within a single taxonomy. There are additional taxonomies available for the user to choose from but the Boolean functionality should work within a single taxonomy or across multiple taxonomies. Also notice how the taxonomy only provides a maximum of three levels of depth.

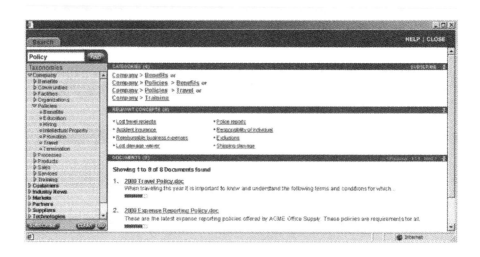

Using Taxonomies to Tag Information

Don't underestimate the power of your taxonomies. Far too many organizations focus on "finding" information and not the categorization of information going "into" a repository. This is a very large mistake. Would you like me to repeat that again for emphasis? This is a very large mistake.

Now that we have used taxonomies to help us "find" information we should also turn around and use the exact same taxonomies to tag information on the way "*into*" a repository. This is so easy and yet has very strategic, long-term benefits. The implementation is still tactical but the results are strategic.

By forcing our users to select a category or two from the taxonomy tree (at least a minimum of one, but preferably as many as they are willing to make) when saving a document, we can employ a hybrid model of manual and automatic categorization. In this essence, we capitalize on the end-user knowing the most relevant categories to bind the document to when they create and save the document (the Yahoo approach), and then we can follow up using our technology to parse the document once its in the repository and find additional relationships. Who knows more about what a document is related to than the document creator?

You get the best of both worlds and the beauty is, it can be integrated into the users daily workflow (note: this is a KM best practice you are witnessing here) and they don't even know they are providing this huge librarian service for the organization.

Tagging information on the way into the repository during the time it is being created is one of the best and least costly methods of both categorizing the information as well as ensuring its accuracy in its binding to the organizational taxonomy.

Taxonomies and Security

Using taxonomies to tag information being created and inserted into the organizational corpus is an exceptional knowledge management best practice.

Unfortunately, when reviewing different types of technologies that can serve the purpose of both tagging on the way in and filtering during a find operation (searching) people will often overlook a major detail incumbent on the technologies: Security.

Remember to keep in mind that search engines often run as services on computers (servers) and have, typically by default, administrative privileges. Even without administrative privileges, these services will need at least a minimum of read-access privileges or the search engines could not get access to all document contents for indexing.

This means that the results of their search could display information that is sensitive to various audiences. Great care needs to be taken in reviewing the security model of any search and categorization technology to make sure it fits with your internal security policies.

Taxonomies as Meta-Data

In knowledge management, there is always lots and lots of talk about generating meta-data standards. Fortunately, by building taxonomies and using the taxonomies to tag data going into the repositories we have, in fact, defined a meta-data standard.

The taxonomy categories can be implemented not only to tag documents but also to tag every piece of transactional data in the enterprise. This means each transactional record could also take advantage of the taxonomy and store categorical information in each record inserted into a database. This methodology would make data warehousing efforts much simpler and transactional information could then be integrated into all other enterprise information for better access to, and analysis of, relationships and relevancy.

Taxonomies as Knowledge Maps

In the field of KM we also always talk about knowledge mapping. Knowledge maps are just another way for us to group logical information about what we know, who knows it and how do we find these people or resources. Knowledge maps are also commonly referred to as organizational "Yellow Pages" or "White pages". In reality, they are just another taxonomy.

Creating a Knowledge Map isn't particularly difficult and makes for a good, inexpensive, KM pilot effort. The problem with knowledge maps is, that they can become stale quite quickly and usually require a good amount of effort keeping them up-to-date. Some people work at it and others don't, so the usefulness can diminish quickly and actually paint a fairly bad picture of your organizations ability to manage itself if the information is not kept current as knowledge maps usually have high visibility. How many times have you looked up a phone number on a website, only to call it and find it changed or disconnected and nobody has bothered to update the directory. This is just bad management.

Therefore, as with other mundane repetitive tasks, it is best to try to automate it using any of the available and up-and-coming mapping technologies. It is also a good idea to dynamically extract names and telephone numbers from your organizations Directory Services as they are usually updated when people move about, enter or leave and organization.

Taxonomies and Classification

Dr. Claude Vogel, Founder & CTO of Semio recently sent me his article dealing with taxonomies and classification. I've been a fan of his Semio Tagger product for years and have used it in practice with great success and have also come to recognize Claude for his contributions to the KM community.

I am pleased to add Claude's article to this book as it aligns with my thoughts and articulates some of the challenges I've personally faced trying to implement KM technological solutions in the past. There is not always an alignment between technology and KM requirements and I think this article exemplifies that.

As a matter of fact, the point Claude is driving at is one of the founding reasons I set about inventing the Decision-Matrix (www.decision-matrix.com)

Fasten your taxonomies; hold on for the classification revolution.

A new generation of information retrieval systems will allow an unprecedented reconciliation of individual creativity and corporate consistency. Next generation information retrieval systems offer a powerful new business model with a potentially huge sociological impact.

Today, there exists the widespread delusion that information progress equals individual appropriation of information. This is simply not the case. Let us examine the progress of corporate information to date. The first age of corporate information systems leaned toward a "big brother" approach, with centralized thesauri and a librarian culture. The second age has been a mix of various attempts to escape the corporate framework and empower individual expertise. Responsibility for knowledge management has been placed in the hands of individuals, using "search it yourself" and "grab-as-you-can" approaches. The reality is that tacit knowledge has not yet been the captured target of any significant corporate deployment.

The third age and next generation information retrieval systems will simultaneously manage critical corporate information assets, while supporting and empowering the very specific problem-solving needs of the individual. The recent explosion in the number of categorization solutions and the improvement in the solutions themselves might be the ferment of a true revolution in corporate information management.

Managing Different and Conflicting Requirements for Information

Information, quite simply, means different things to different audiences. Corporations view information as an entity, an asset that needs to be organized, maintained and possibly displayed through a portal or content management system. Individuals however view information as a means to an end. The value of information to an individual is temporal and dynamic, whereas corporations value information as a long-lasting, tangible asset.

At the very heart of any information management strategy you must acknowledge and address the significant disconnect between the requirements of the two primary information audiences–the corporation and the individual. You must also address the fact that despite their very different needs, both audiences will perceive that they have the same problem–the inability to access the information they seek.

Good Corporate Solutions Exist

Corporation information management strategy typically includes some combination of the use of portals, content management systems, navigation tools and search technology.

The philosophy shared by each of these technologies is their focus on corporate management of information. These systems gather vast amounts of information from different sources and repositories and make it available, in a neutral and uniform fashion, to employees.

More sophisticated companies employ content categorization and indexing as a critical component of their corporate information management strategy. Indexing establishes a foundation for corporate information management by establishing an agreed upon and understood hierarchy of information organization. The structure of this categorized information, optimally reflected in a taxonomy, reflects the corporation's view of its world.

Since these taxonomies reflect a collective view, they tend to be top-down and librarian-driven. Resulting information, once it has been uniformly categorized and organized, is presented en masse to employees through an interface of some sort–a simple viewer, a portal, etc. These are positive attributes that support the stability and accessibility of information at a corporate level.

Corporate management and presentation of information is critical. In addition to managing a tangible asset (information), these systems enable explicit access to a collective representation of useful information. They have the additional and harder to quantify benefits of providing a corporation with an identity, a unifying mechanism, and clarification of corporate views.

So, why do knowledge workers still perceive that they either have difficulty accessing information or experience information overload? Why do portals, effectively and expensively implemented, typically have such low traffic rates despite providing single point access to vast volumes of corporate data? Such portal traffic figures provide a clue that something isn't quite right. Information access has been arguably provided, but it is not perceived as solving day-to-day problems for individuals.

The bottom line is that corporate portals do address top-line information management issues but they do not begin to address the information requirements of the individual. Information has been organized, but it hasn't made the transition to knowledge valued by individuals. To support the specific knowledge needs of the individual, you need a new model that uses the existing corporate information model as its foundation.

A New Information Model

The new information model sits on top of the corporate presentation of data that has been carefully collected, categorized and managed. This basic information management strategy must begin with an understanding of the data itself.

The contents of each data source—whether it is an e-mail or research report—must be understood and uniquely indexed. Indexing and resulting ontologies establish a foundation for classification. Powerful indexing tools such as SemioTagger use a sophisticated, patented combination of linguistic analysis techniques matched to a customized taxonomy to understand, extract and uniquely index the key concepts of documents. This "universal" indexing level is very important. It creates a foundation, a level of corporate consistency, on which you can build. It also is granular enough to support the dynamic generation of wildly varying views or slices of data.

"Universal" doesn't mean one enormous ontology covering all possible topics. For a lot of reasons, it's better to envision the foundation as a collection of vertical (legal, pharmaceutical, etc.) and horizontal (Financial, Marketing, etc.) ontologies. Some of these structures will have a full ontological power: they will define the basic components of a given world, as in "our vision of the financial world." Others will just recapitulate in a nomenclature the parts and subparts of well accepted mechanisms: geographical names, company products, etc.

When we say that "universal indexing" will be the foundation of corporation assets, we are emphasizing the collective vision embedded in
these representations. It is likely that such consensual representations
will expand outside of the corporation and likewise influence incoming
information. This is the reason why specialized librarians and knowledge workers will have the protected responsibility to manage these
ontologies. They have the stratospheric vision, the detachment from
day-to-day foibles, which keeps them dedicated to corporate-level
thinking.

This all sounds reasonable. But now we must turn back to reality, it's a
tough world out there with urgencies, passions, and a whole pandemo-
nium of creative forces. The good news is that, because we have done
such a good job at building high-level ontologies, we can now more easily address idiosyncrasies.

What Individuals Need

Problem-Solving Support
In sharp contrast to corporate information management—which must
be stable, uniform and understandable at a collective level—individuals
need very specific information, organized in a way that makes intuitive
sense to them alone. Individuals don't care about the "system" as long as
it works for them. Individuals don't need to see the underlying ontologies. They want precise views of information on their desktop, categorized in a way that lets them resolve very specific problems.

Again, in contrast to the corporate model, a system serving individuals
must have a bottom-up orientation. Classification becomes important.
Information can be *indexed* at a corporate level, but it must be *classified*
at the individual or community level.

Indexing of concepts structured in ontologies sets a base level of stable, manageable and maintainable metacontent. Classification of concepts, however, are individualistic and temporary. They need to address the shifting needs of an individual or community. They help end users make sense of tagged information by allowing it to be looked at from any oddball matrix of ideas. The value of classification is in the *connections* between seemingly disparate data, and it is these connections that must be captured using new and different structures and processes.

In summary, information indexing is:

➢ Focused on corporate objectives

➢ Librarian-driven

➢ Top-down, collective

➢ Reflective or collective, corporate culture

➢ Representative of neutral, non-conflictive view of data

➢ Based on unique, mono-paradigm sets of assumptions

➢ Stable, slow-growing

➢ Focused on concepts, structured in ontology's

➢ Critical as the foundation of any information management system

Whereas classification is:

➢ Designed for individual problem-solving

➢ Librarian, expert or final user driven

➢ Pragmatic, bottom-up

➢ Addresses individual or small community's needs

➢ Idiosyncratic

➢ Inconsistent and conflictual

➢ Unstable

> Focuses on a cross-perspective matrix
> Dependent upon stable, categorization system

Consider a specific example. Individuals seek information in order to address very specific problems. In the case of a pharmaceutical company, a scientist or research group may be attempting to develop a drug for treating Alzheimer's. An "expert" in the field will not want to see every piece of data known about Alzheimer's or spend time keying in every possible query combination to view across-the-board information. Most likely the expert already has grounding in the type of information such research would provide. Instead the expert may wish to view all genes with a known relationship to Alzheimer's or all drugs that have a known effect of some sort on Alzheimer's. Once this cross section of information has been examined, the researcher may then wish to view the information in a different way using a different priority, or add yet another matrix to the information mix–say a particular age group or nationality.

The point is that the scientist wants to find and structure desktop information according to their specific thinking at that moment. The expert will find an answer or at least a pattern somewhere in a constantly progressing cross section of information. Dynamic presentation of very specific information is critical. People do this naturally in a variety of unconscious ways. But as the quantity of data available surpasses the ability of even our remarkable brains, some kind of support tool will become increasingly critical.

How Information Classification Benefits Companies

Classification helps companies because it empowers the creative, intuitive and deductive thought processes of its knowledge workers.

Classification enables the dynamic presentation of dimensions of data uniquely created by the knowledge worker. By enabling workers to turn information around, inside out, viewed from this way and that, with new dimensions added and taken away, you enable discovery.

Classification also provides a framework for collaboration between individuals and between communities. While an individual may make a specific discovery, progress will nearly always follow based on the social dynamics of an expert group. To date, companies have seen the final results of this type of social exchange, but the activity leading to the results could also generate very useful data.

Corporations must value and support individual efforts and small discoveries, with a manageable way of making these discoveries available to relevant parties for further research. Outside of the considerable benefits of empowering individual creativity, collaboration has clearly been shown to improve corporate efficiency. By reducing duplication of effort and enabling simultaneous, real-time design of multiple product or drug components, effective collaboration reduces design, research and development time and brings products to buyers faster.

New Sociological Model As Well

Progress is made through interaction and challenges. Any pragmatic model put together by one expert will most likely be useful to other experts in the field. Information tools serving individuals should also be designed to serve the needs of communities or groups of like-minded individuals. Support for individual problem solving therefore must be expanded to include support for collaborative problem solving. And here the level of complexity grows again.

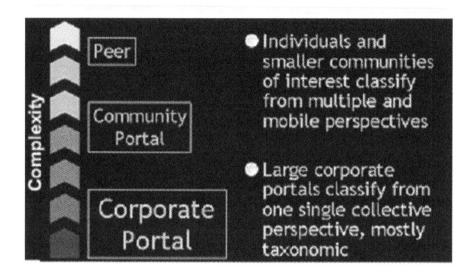

For example, the real value of a subset of information may lie in how it is combined or in the model used to access or view that particular slice of information. Experts should be able to store, adapt, borrow, merge and share data models. Making this information available to others, through push or pull technology, is another critical element of classification.

Conclusion

Corporate information and individual knowledge are related and inter-dependent. And yet the processes required to manage each function are antithetical. Again, many companies have done a good job of organizing and managing their corporate information assets. But in doing so, they have not yet addressed the specific information needs of the individual. In high tech and research-oriented organizations in particular, the costs of inhibiting individual creativity or not capturing discovery processes are significant.

Information classification is a means of empowering the individual by providing them with flexible, dynamic and complete access to very specific information. The process is complex. It requires a new way of viewing data–new information and sociological models. It requires the provision of a virtual "hyper-cube" of information, spinning and changing and evolving in lockstep with the individual's thought process. But the rewards and the benefits to corporations are vast. With classification, information truly becomes a tool. And corporations can manage a process of empowering, analyzing, capturing and sharing the incremental work of its most valuable employees.

(www.semio.com)

Chapter 7 Best Practices

Here is where I'm going to get into trouble.

Most of my career has been spent re-engineering governments and commercial organizations, from the very, very big to mid-size.

On many occasions, I, and others around me have tried to capture best practices and disseminate them for the betterment of the organization.

On several occasions (yes, more than once) these attempts failed.

Sad to say, but true non-the-less.

So I set about analyzing "why?" so I could understand the rules that we needed to follow to ensure a better level of success. I've explored a multitude of case examples on the use and management of best practices, yet I couldn't achieve satisfactory level of success. I would rate "success" as being the full adoption, acceptance, integration and on-going application of a best practice.

So when I was contemplating what works and what failed, I thought deeply about what I knew worked and worked very well. There was one predominantly area of best practices that has never failed me; the best practice around team building! This works every single place I implement it.

So after all of the research and real-life trials and failures I will now tell you what I believe, at this moment in time.

For the most part, capturing best practices is a waste of time.

Yes, that's right: a waste of time….but keep reading…

If you work in the field of KM you are probably gagging on that last statement, as there are many testimonials about the successful application of best practices.

Why then, do I say that it's a waste of time?

For one main reason: Knowledge workers basically want to do it themselves.

Yes, there are plenty of good reasons why they should follow someone else's best practices, but the primary motivator to "do it themselves" overrules the good reasons. What reward is there in doing things someone else's way? Where is the novelty, the satisfaction or the personal payback? There isn't, and knowledge workers know it.

Remember, as I stated much earlier, knowledge workers don't really care about the company (I know that is hard to hear but it's true), they're almost totally consumed by challenge and pier respect.

Implementing someone else's solution doesn't present a challenge and doesn't generate much respect. It's good for the company but not necessarily the knowledge worker.

If this is the case then why have there been successful cases of best practice implementation (according to stories told by others)?

Here's one simple answer. If you invent a best practice, you can ensure its success if you're the CEO and can stuff it down everyone's throat (or to put it more politely, to delegate with authority). I know this for certain, because I've done it.

But is this really an answer to the problem? Well, that depends on the severity of the problem you are trying to solve. If its sink or swim time, then by all means, you do what you have to do.

Is it sustainable? No.

You can force things in an emergency, but on the whole, this type of implementation doesn't go over very well, and the required on-going drive to keep the best practice in operation is difficult to maintain. On top of all that, not everyone is a CEO, so it is a very limiting technique.

Now that I've disclosed this piece of knowledge, go back and have a closer look at those attractive case studies. What you will find is that a great many of these "tributes" to Best Practices that you come across are usually CEO driven and are usually paradigm-shifts in organizational process. Follow up on them a year later and most people will have no idea what you're talking about.

I remember one time not long ago when the CEO of a high tech company I worked for politely requested a best practices initiative around software application security. This came right from the top so each department had to cooperate and we assembled a cross-functional team that would build a best practice model for all departments to implement.

We were successful in building the best practice and getting it distributed to the field. The CEO then sent out a directive telling everyone to implement this and they did…for a while.

You see, the CEO did what he knew had to be done, made the right decisions and pushed the best practice into place. And it worked…for a while.

But that's where it stopped. The CEO went on to other challenges having solved this one and got consumed on larger issues. His attention was diverted. Managers came and went and no one was left the ownership of the best practice.

Within 12 months I personally witnessed an entirely new initiative starting from several new department heads in a grassroots type movement to start developing a new software security best practice for the organization.

I couldn't believe what I saw. I sat back and watched for a bit while emails flew back and forth and meetings were held and decisions were contemplated.

Just before things got too far out of hand I sent out a broadcast email to everyone that was participating on this new committee and asked them "Did you realize this has all been done before? Did anyone even bother looking in our knowledgebase?"

There was a dramatic pause of the committee and you could audibly hear a pin drop. Then the communications began to fly. Everyone felt completely stupid and tried desperately to avoid being associated with this effort. After all, this was a large high tech company that goes around expounding their proficiencies in Knowledge Management. The CEO just laughed and shook his head, but the point was made.

As you can see, even the best intentions will be for naught if they are not driven, driven and continue to be driven. The very second that momentum dies the knowledge virtually disappears into oblivion.

The knowledge worker culture demands we build new and shiny things constantly. To avoid this and implement a sustainable best practices model we need to do the following:

1. Senior management must pick targets (only pick one per senior executive until he or she can handle two)

2. Senior management must advocate the best practice initiative

3. Senior management must drive the best practice

4. Senior management must continue to enforce and reward the application of the best practice

5. Senior management must not let the best practice drop off their radar, unless they no longer need it, because it will surely disappear in an instant.

6. Senior management should choose a formal abandonment strategy because best practices come and go and shouldn't be carried any further than they're worth (set metrics).

7. Senior management should implement the "Team Structure" best practice I spoke of earlier because it works and is the only truly

self-governing best practice that accommodates knowledge worker culture that I have ever found.

8. Senior management should implement the Decision-Matrix (as discussed in the chapter called "Communities of Practice") as a way of pushing best practices out into the enterprise.

9. The application of best practices should be designed into the workers daily workflow to make it unnoticeable if possible.

10.The application of best practices should become part of the employees performance review process.

So after grabbing your attention at the beginning of this chapter by saying:

"For the most part, capturing best practices is a waste of time"

I will now alter that statement to summarize what I really meant:

For the most part, capturing best practices is a waste of time IF SENIOR MANAGEMENT DOESN'T DRIVE THE BEST PRACTICE INITIA-TIVE AND MAINTAIN THE VIGILANCE.

Ok, so I misled you a bit at the beginning, but it helped make the point I was trying to get across, didn't it.

Chapter 8 Communities of Practice

Everyone in the world is building glorious Communities of Practice.-
Just joking.

No really, there is more hype about CoP's than just about anything else
in knowledge management. Why? The answer is simple: there are
numerous shrink-wrap products you can buy, stick on a server somewhere, point your browser at it, and "technologically" they work. As for
a return on your investment, that's another story.

Much like a best practice, the CoP is typically implemented to solve a
particular problem, and mark my words; it requires the exact same
management style as "best practice management". Force it into place,
measure it, monitor it, keep enforcing and rewarding participation, set
metrics and develop an abandonment strategy.

So what is a Community of Practice?

**Simply put, a CoP is a virtual workspace where people with similar
interests or issues can get together and collaborate.**

And to put practice back into theory: **A CoP is a Knowledge Broker**

Let's have a look at some of the constituent parts that make up a good
CoP. For a case example I intend to use the Community of Practice software developed by non-other than myself.

The software is called "Decision-Matrix"
Here is the URL: http://www.decision-matrix.com

Decision-Matrix Community of Practice

OK, let's pick a "universal" problem and implement a Community of Practice to fix it. Remember that we implement tactical solutions to resolve definable problems.

Let's start right off by stating the nature of the problem:

> *Providing appropriate information is limited*
> *by our ability to ask the right questions.*

In technology today we have a heavy emphasis on providing copious quantities of information hoping it will help users draw correct conclusions to questions. The problem with this type of service is that we are not assisting users by helping guide them through a full Frid Decision Cycle. It is the nature of humans to sacrifice accuracy in favor of speed. Providing large amounts of information does not necessarily increase the probability of successful decisions.

Better decisions made faster equals better bottom line and greater innovation, both being key ingredients for survival. Computers aren't intelligent; people are, so if someone asks a question the computer will provide data accordingly. But what if the questions are either wrong or not encompassing enough to provide enough granularity or don't factor interrelated components of the issue? The results will catch people by surprise and vary greatly in their impact on the outcome.

To help prevent surprise outcomes we introduce processes such as risk, opportunity, issue and change management. These are great tools for contingency planning and execution but are, in effect, the "pound of cure" instead of the "ounce of prevention". Prevention needs to take place during the initial Frid Decision-Cycle.

So how do we do that? We could always have our senior experienced people generate a list of every single question they can contrive that must be asked in a given situation. That would be a start, but it becomes quickly apparent that the numbers of variables are huge and some variables are obviously (and some not so obviously) more important than others. If we approached decision-making in this linear fashion, then the time consumed could prove daunting. Remembering that humans prefer fast information, this type of system would soon fall by the wayside or become outdated as variables change with time and circumstance, and the cost of maintenance would prove prohibitive.

We are faced with a task, to ensure that our users are asking the right questions. A "list" of questions fails to accommodate an understanding of relationships other than rudimentary clustering (sales type questions, technical type questions, etc.). A list of questions is also too static and too time consuming to generate and maintain.

Fictional Case Example

ABCco employs 300 workers in different facets of the manufacturing organization. This company has an annual budget of $10M to develop new product and service offerings in order to remain competitive and stimulate growth. The management staff is regularly confronted with employees telling them they have a great idea that the company should look at to see if it's worth exploring.

The company faces a problem. None of the ideas are ever presented in a consistent format so it takes management a significant amount of time to consider each idea. When presented, the ideas are also never researched sufficiently and there is a lot of work that management must do to come to a better understanding of the implications of these ideas.

With several hundred employees randomly presenting ideas it can consume a significant amount of time and resources exploring every idea. This time and energy usually rests on the shoulders of the senior executives, as they are typically the people with enough business experience to understand the many implications that surround and impact new opportunities.

Management has for many years been attempting to push decision making down throughout the enterprise, but it's this lack of business experience in junior employees that hampers such efforts. How can you expect a specialized machinist or engineer to understand the impact of their idea on cash flow or the balance sheet? What is the likelihood they would understand the impact of global or local economics on their idea?

The bottom line is, that they just don't have enough experience to even know what questions to ask. This type of experience doesn't come cheap. It's usually those individuals that have had to run their own companies or at least managed their divisions accounting, marketing, sales, engineering and services, that have fought the fights, won and lost battles, and have learned over time from the school of hard knocks which wars to fight and which ones to avoid. This experience is not something easily handed down in a company or mentored to the general population of an organization.

Yet we still have the need to assess every potential opportunity that can present itself. This leaves us in a conundrum. We want our employees to do the work analyzing new opportunities and remove roadblocks that would frustrate them in presenting new ideas. Yet, those individuals that have the experience to understand the ramifications of potential ideas are the senior executives and they are few and far between, usually with little time to spare.

When it comes time to allocate that $10M the executives need to assemble whatever ideas they've had time to research, estimate the impact to the company, project a return on investment and then spend the time to figure out which of the potentially hundreds of ideas presented are the best ideas to invest in. Each executive in turn will usually present their ideas in a format they have grown accustomed to and no two executives will present in the exact same fashion because even they have strengths and weaknesses and usually assess ideas from the perspectives of their own experiences.

This is where the Decision-Matrix comes in.

The Decision-Matrix presents users with a consistent method of exploring ideas and mitigating risks by using a question-based approach to research. Each idea will be run through a Patent-Pending matrix of questions whose interrelationships and relevancies have been predetermined. Each aspect of an idea is broken into divisions within the matrix and each question within each division receives a score based on its impact on other questions.

The Decision-Matrix allows a user to navigate through a gauntlet of questions that they should be asking, but perhaps never even thought about before now. While they are answering questions they're also creating, with simple point-and-click actions, initial revenue potential estimates, capital requirements and cash flow projections. They have no need to understand accounting, just whether or not they think a question requires money and whether or not it will make or save money.

The Decision-Matrix doesn't answer the questions for them; it really wants to know whether someone has spent time thinking about all the issues and whether or not they have factored in all the criteria that someone will need to approve the idea. Its purpose is to mitigate risk.

After all, mitigating risk and increasing the odds of probability are what decision-making is all about.

The Decision-Matrix provides a weighted scoring system that allows users to see how they are doing in each section in terms of probability.

Probability is a measurement of confidence. The Decision-Matrix also allows management to input rules, thresholds, and triggers that can help guide and affect the user during the Frid Decision Cycle. Therefore you have a best practices capturing system built right in.

At the end of the day, when ideas are presented to management, they are packaged in a consistent report that provides all the background research, scores, level of confidence associated with every issue, and a preliminary or detailed financial model that demonstrates the capital requirements, earnings potential and cash flow.

The users themselves, instead of consuming large quantities of senior management time, have now performed the majority of the research. The reports themselves are now consistent with each other and can be measured very quickly to assess which ideas offer the best return and what level of risk there is with each. Senior management can now quickly filter the available list of ideas to find those that best suit their budget and organizational fit. All ideas are also archived in the matrix for future reference.

All departmental Decision-Matrix databases have been completely denormalized for easy aggregation into Data Warehouses and Decision-Support systems for pattern and trending analysis.

The illustration below shows us a system that provides a relational taxonomy of questions bound in a multi-dimensional matrix that predefines relationships based on the patent-pending probability engine.

The scores you see not only analyze the weights of each relationship but also integrate the risks and issues into the overall scoring system as additional factors.

The result is a systematic method for reducing risk in any venture.

Decision Matrix Probability Assessment Engine:

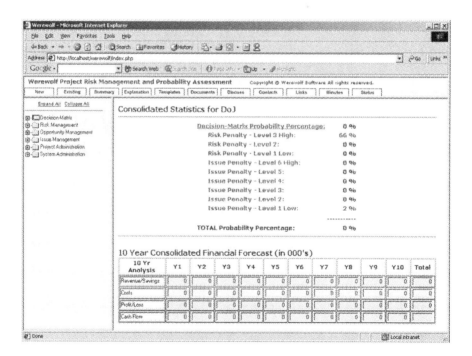

RISK Management Controls

The Decision-Matrix Risk Management Control Center automates Risk Management tasks while building a real-time knowledgebase of valuable lessons learned for future reference by other projects and personnel.

- **Threat Analysis**
- **Contingency Planning**
- **Notification Services**
- **Escalation**
- **Action Items**

Decision-Matrix Risk Management Engine:

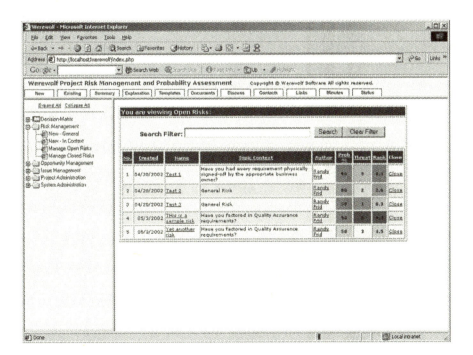

OPPORTUNITY Management Controls

In the exact same fashion as a Risk, Opportunities may present themselves or loom on the horizon and offer potential for integration into your project. All of the factors are basically the same as a risk only inversely proportional. The Decision-Matrix Risk Management Control Center automates Opportunity Management tasks in a similar fashion to Risk Management only inversely proportional.

- Benefit Analysis
- Contingency Planning
- Notification Services
- Action Items

ISSUE Management Controls

When a Risk becomes reality it is now an Issue. Issues must be resolved or you stand the chance of jeopardizing your project to a degree dependent on the nature of the Issue. Issues present themselves as a "real" danger to your project. The Decision-Matrix Issue Management Control Center automates Issue Management tasks in a similar fashion to Risk and Opportunity Management.

- Threat Analysis
- Contingency Planning
- Notification Services
- Escalation
- Action Items

Threaded Discussions

An all time favorite. A place to have text-based conversations that multiple people can participate in. The business benefit of this type of discussion board is that the knowledge is stored in a knowledge-base and can typically be searched and reviewed.

Threaded discussions typically allow the users to monitor all the discussions that take place and to participate at will. Some discussion forums will also allow users to "subscribe" to a thread so that notification of changes will be automatically sent to them via email.

Threaded Discussion forum:

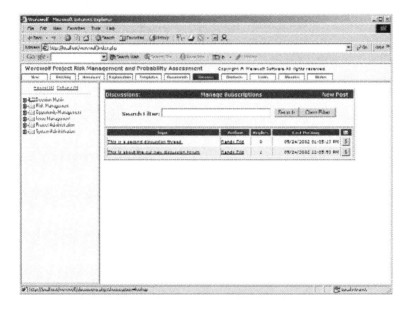

Document Management

Document Management is an absolute essential ingredient for CoP collaboration. A way of clustering and tagging documents that are relevant to the subject matter of the community. Since most CoP's utilize web-based technologies (primarily for convenience), they will also typically utilize the browser to upload and view on-line documents.

Document Management:

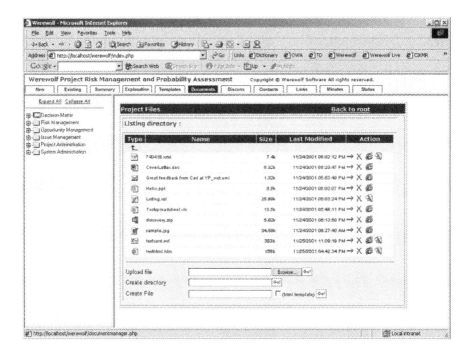

Link Management

Link (URL) management is something a typical CoP will provide so that users can enter external or internal links to documents, websites, etc., that they have found useful.

Link Management:

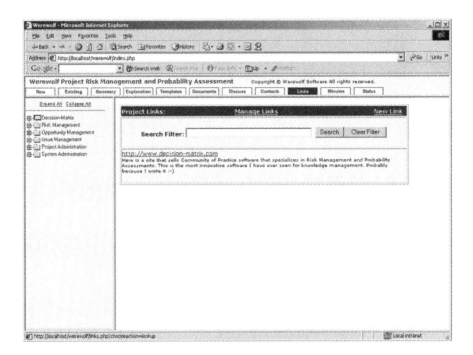

Contact Management

Contact management is like link management and will provide CoP users a way to share an external or internal directory of contacts relevant to the community.

Contact Management:

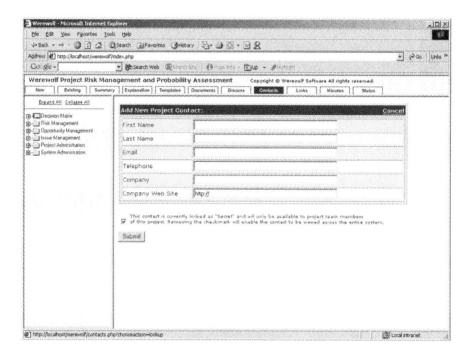

Minutes of the Meetings

A very nice feature to have is a CoP module that stores minutes of meetings. These are usually brainstorming sessions and have assigned action items. Usually this information gets discarded or is managed somewhere else. This keeps all the associated meeting knowledge in the same place as the rest of the CoP.

Minutes of the Meetings:

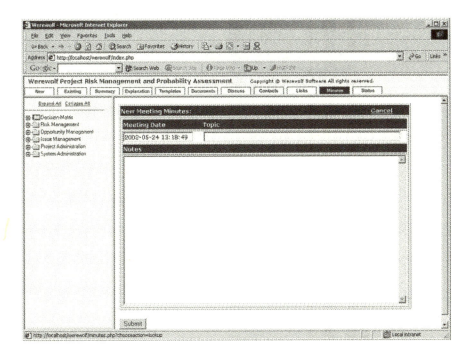

Status Update Reports

As with the meeting minutes module, it is a nice feature to allow the entry and storage of Status Reports. These are usually individual items and become a great source of finding Subject Matter Experts (SME).

Status Update Reports:

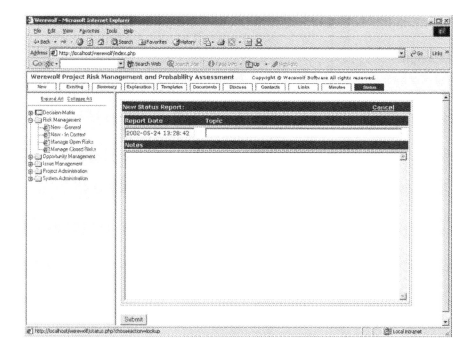

Chapter 9–Building a KM Program

This chapter assumes that your organization is pushing to engage "Knowledge Management" even though, in all probability, most senior directors really have no idea what KM is all about. Therefore they have assigned you to figure it out and "make it happen".

So what you need to do is figure out what to build to kick off the KM Program that will have reasonable cross-functional visibility, produce quick results and be fairly easy to take on and complete with a very small budget. If you are in the same boat as most other organizations, the management wants KM but they don't want to spend any money (at least not until the numbers are in).

So we need to pick some "low hanging fruit" for an easy win on the first pilot.

I would suggest implementing either a Community of Practice (CoP) or a Knowledge Map (also referred to as corporate yellow pages). Both are good.

But, before we can do that we need to:

1. Pick a problem you want to solve

2. Understand the structure of a KM program

3. Get the CKO role defined and someone in that position

4. Define the mission statement, and

5. Perform a Knowledge assessment

Developing a Project Charter

Since all projects are different, what I will do is provide you with a typical Table of Contents and you can fill in the rest.

Project Overview

> - Project Purpose
> - Project Scope
> - Project Objectives
> - Outstanding Issues
> - Approvals
> - References
> - Terminology

Project Approach

> - Project Deliverables and Quality Objectives
> - Organization, Responsibilities & Project Org Chart
> - Dependencies
> - Plans for Support Activities
>   - o Project training
>   - o Technical reviews
>   - o Documentation support
>   - o Status monitoring
>   - o Communications plan (see next section)
>   - o Contract and procurement management

- Project Facilities and Resource Requirements
- Risk Management
- Process Options and Deviations
- Stages
- Project Control
    - *Project management tools*
        - *(i.e. Decision-Matrix, RUP, MSF, etc.)*
    - *Risk, Opportunity, Issue and Change management*
    - *Activity reports*
    - *Team leader meetings*
    - *Project meetings*
    - *Project progress reports*
- Quality Control Activities
- Project Schedule
- Project Effort Estimate
- Project Cost Estimate
- Appendices

The Project Charter should also contain some type of document version control table like the following:

Document Change Control

Version #	Date of Issue	Author(s)	Brief Description of Change
1.0	22 Dec 2001	G. Zilla	Preliminary draft to facilitate planning and information collection
1.1	15 Jan 2002	J. Daniels	Draft for consultation with project sponsor and ABC officials
1.2	19 Jan 2002	M. Mouse	Draft incorporating the comments from ABC and departmental officials that were received 18 Jan 2002

Communication Plan

A KM project must have a communication plan. Remember, in Phase 1 we are primarily advocating the project so the communication program is an important aspect.

The objective of building a communication plan is awareness, support and acceptance of the project among key audiences.

A successful communication plan should:

> ➤ Send tailored messages that are strategic, tactical and personal.

    o Strategic
        ▪ Why are we doing this?
        ▪ Why is it important?
        ▪ What are the long-term benefits?
    o Tactical
        ▪ Project status (who, what, when, where, how)

O Personal

■ What's in for me?

➤ Ensure communication is coming from the top

➤ Share ideas as soon as possible instead of waiting for completion

➤ Encourage dialog and feedback

Details of the plan should include:

➤ Target audiences
➤ Tailored messages
➤ Best method of communicating each message
➤ People responsible for communicating
➤ Timeframe of communications

Your project manager can also develop a simple communication log file to keep track:

Timeframe	Audience	Method	Responsibility	Message
3/01/02	CoP Engineers	Email	M. Mouse	Project commencement
4/01/02	CoP User Community	Presentation	J. Daniels	Project presentation, benefits
1/05/03	CoP User Community	Email	G. Zilla	Launch day approaches

Managing the KM Program Project

As with any project, it is very important that there is a clear course of action defined throughout its life cycle. I have seen more projects fail because of poor project management than for any other reason.

It is for that reason that this section will explore the concept of a simple project framework, what is a framework, why we need one, and how it works. I had to make a decision that there was value in discussing this subject as there are ample books on project management on the market that describe simple to complex strategies for managing projects and this book is focused on knowledge management. But the bottom line is, that a project management framework is really a formal methodology for collecting and disseminating explicit knowledge and identifying tacit knowledge resources.

The framework is relatively simple. It's broken into four concepts: The Trinity, Management Controls, Proxy Reporting and Post Implementation Review. I'll go over each one in turn.

Before we begin, many of you reading this may have run projects in the past and may be wondering why I'm not talking about Waterfall Methodology, Iterative Processes or Rapid Development. These are methods of executing project staging over the life cycle of the project. Some methods are simply step-by-step, others require systematic feedback loops, and others leap ahead of the final deliverable by delivering pieces into production to test their viability throughout the development.

These systems of project deployment are well documented and debated in project management journals everywhere and most importantly are all included in the Trinity. There's no need for me to decide which system is best as they all have a place in managing projects and any of them work within the scope of the Trinity.

The four framework components I'll speak of are used for measurement and communication.

The Trinity

The cornerstone of the four project management framework components is the Trinity.

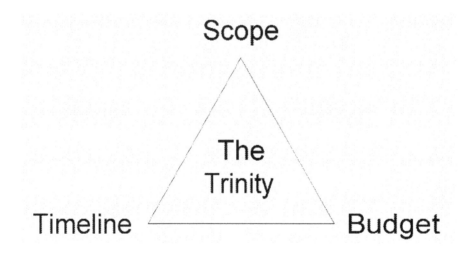

As the drawing indicates, the Trinity is concerned with putting a management wrapper around the three physical aspects of any project: the scope, timeline and budget.

Although the Trinity is extremely important for project managers it is far more important that everyone use this fundamental tool to manage their everyday projects of every size. It's simple and effective and makes people think before acting. Before anyone goes off and starts a project (small or large) it should be required that he or she file a Trinity plan with their manager. Even if it's on one piece of paper or a napkin, the real purpose is the process of actually writing down ones intentions and testing those intentions against a predetermined scope, budget and timeline. It makes people accountable for their actions.

Scope

Scope is the most important thing to focus on as a project manager. Scope "creep" is when your project starts as one thing and then blossoms into something else without anyone really paying attention to the ramifications. This is classic on large projects and in large organizations. Once someone gets some money approved for a project, others try to get other work done that really has little to do with the original project, and bleed funds from the project to pay for it. Others decide that certain features just "must" be added to take advantage of this or that opportunity and the feature list just grows and grows because the enhancements look so small and trivial that project members just agree to it. Eventually these minor enhancements aggregate into very significant time expenditures and the Trinity is blown.

So how do we manage scope?

1. Create a Project Charter that outlines why this project is happening and what benefits it could offer?
2. Define the business requirements
3. Create a detailed project plan with carefully defined deliverables
4. Carefully define Roles and Responsibilities
5. Bind the project under the watchful eye of the Management Controls we will be talking about in this chapter.

Timeline

You track timelines for obvious reasons. For tracking a timeline you can use something like Microsoft Project. Scope creep most often generates Timeline deviations.

Later we will talk about risk management. In reality, if you spend the majority of your time managing risks you will find that your timeline management is simple.

Why?

Because a timeline defines the deliverables and tasks to be performed, so long as you have your Subject Matter Experts assemble their respective timeline task estimates then the only thing that will ever deviate the timeline is a risk that has become reality (when a risk becomes an issue).

Therefore, by performing proper risk management on every timeline item, you can identify the risks ahead of time and build in a contingency plan for each risk. In this fashion you can predict any deviations to the timeline in advance.

This allows you to model two timelines; one timeline is a best-case scenario and the other is a worst-case scenario. You can then use the deltas between the two timelines to understand the project's minimum and maximum time, scope and budget requirements.

Budget

Another obvious thing you must track. This is where you define every single thing that is going to cost money during a project (I do mean everything). Once you've guessed at everything that could drain your coffers, you factor in a contingency amount to cover the costs you can't guess, as these will always appear (I know, that sounds pessimistic). Budget deviations are most often generated by scope creep. Notice the similarity to timeline problems.

Management Controls

So why did I skip through the Timeline and Budget sections so quickly? Because you can learn that stuff anywhere. What's more important for knowledge management efforts are the Management Controls.

What are the management controls? Take a look at the following diagram and you'll see the flow of knowledge from one management control to the next:

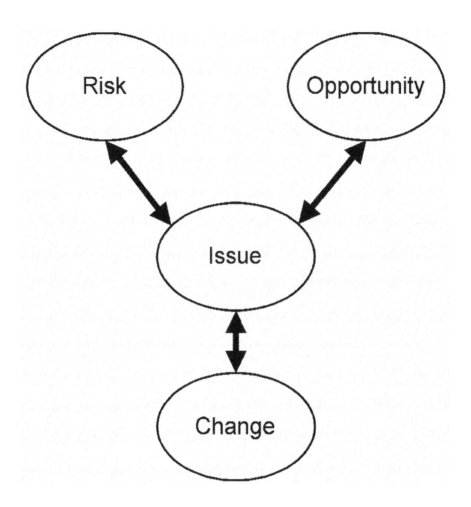

As you can see, Risks and Opportunities escalate to become Issues, and Issues escalate to Change management for resolution.

1. Risk Management

If you decide you don't want to use many different management controls and will only ever use one, than this is the one. This is where our Tacit knowledge comes shining through. Risk management is part of the formal project management framework and is designed to stimulate, escalate and capture risk-associated knowledge. At each stage of a risks life cycle we store its properties, state and assignments. These are retained in our knowledge management systems as a "lessons learned" library.

Risks are potentially harmful exposures that we forecast using our years of experience in determination of everything that can possibly go wrong, from the obvious to the subtle. Conditions in which the project exists, including political, demographic, and economic, etc. have an impact on your potential success or failure. Since change is constant, then our knowledge management concerns are to capture the risks and identify whoever has had experience with similar issues and may be able to offer input on how to resolve them. Identifying our concerns well in advance gives us significant leverage to protect against them.

The process of Risk escalation is simple. Here's the rule of thumb:

1. If it's low risk then you just assign it and monitor it.
2. If it's medium risk then you assign it, monitor it and develop a contingency plan
3. High risks follow the same process as medium risks except that if a high risk reaches 100% then it escalates to a issue automatically and must be resolved right away

You can manage risks (and all the other controls as well) by using an automated program or you can use a simple logbook. It doesn't really matter so long as you manage it. Of course, from a knowledge management perspective it would be better to store this information digitally so it can participate in the knowledgebase. Hard copy makes things very difficult to search and retrieve later on.

Microsoft Exchange and Lotus Notes are particularly excellent products to build automated management controls upon because the asynchronous form-based workflow capabilities are exactly what management control escalation systems take full advantage of. You can also build a risk log just using a word processor or spreadsheet. You can also build a web-enabled application that uses a database back-end to store the information.

Whichever way you choose to develop and implement the management controls is much less important that enforcing their use through policy and training. It will obviously cost more initially to develop a database system as compared to a simple electronic document, but the long-term savings if you intend to use it for more than one project will be worth the time.

Storing the data in a database has the added benefit of allowing you to write business rules into the logic that can perform the escalation automatically and forward the high-level issues to those that require the information. Your business rules become workflow rules that lend themselves very well to technologies such as web applications, messaging workflow systems and directory services.

Here is a sample risk log legend:

ITEM	The Item Number of the Risk being analyzed
RISK	The Risk being analyzed
S–Scope	What is the possibility of this Risk affecting the scope?
$-Budget	What is the possibility of this Risk affecting the budget?
T–Timeline	What is the possibility of this Risk affecting the timeline?
O–Opportunities	What is the possibility of this Risk affecting the opportunities?
R	The overall Rating of the Risk
L	**Low impact**-(Requires Monitoring–Project Proceeds)
M	**Medium Impact**-(Requires Contingency Plan–Project Proceeds)
H	**High Impact**-(Resolution Required Immediately)

Item	Risk	Date	S	$	T	O	R	Action Taken
1	Technology will change throughout the life of this project	7/15/99	M	M	M	M	M	Assigned to Bob. Develop contingency plan that will address the potential changes to technology and a strategy to minimize impact. Setup on-going monitoring.
2	Equipment may arrive late	7/15/99	L	M	H	L	H	Assigned to Mary. High risk because of weather conditions within the state. Late equipment delivery will defer deployment to branches.
3	Computer Room upgrades not completed on-time	7/19/99	L	M	H	L	M	Assigned to Jane. Contingency would be to build production machines in a different room and move in when completed. Power and cabling will be required in temporary room.
4	A Project team member may become absent or leave the project	7/30/99	L	L	L	L	L	Assigned to Jim. Identify additional resources to retrofit team when necessary.

2. Opportunity Management

Opportunity management is the inverse of Risk management. We can easily recognize that over the length of a large project things will change. This is especially true in the Information Technology field. As new products or revisions come available, as politics, economics and demographics change, we need to assess whether or not we should take advantage of the new change or will it set us back so much that it will significantly effect the Trinity.

The Opportunity log and/or program work exactly the same as the Risk log/program. The major difference is that Opportunities are not part of determination of a projects viability. In other words, we typically build a project on its own merits without assessing opportunities that don't exist. As opportunities come along we may or may not take advantage of them depending on how they effect the Trinity and their potential return. If we choose to ignore or never take advantage of an opportunity then the project is still viable. On the other hand if we choose to ignore a risk it could affect the viability of the entire project if it comes to fruition.

From a knowledge management perspective it is important to capture opportunities as they represent one of the most important aspects of knowledge management, the stimulation, identification and capturing of innovation in the enterprise.

Sometimes, throughout a project, we lose track of opportunities that present themselves without a systematic approach to opportunity management. Without a management system these opportunities will drift into nowhere and get forgotten. Building software to automate escalation of opportunities, to consolidate and report on opportunities, and to send reminders at specific times based on thresholds and events are ways we can capitalize on technology to participate in a knowledge management system. Capturing these thoughts into a formal database will preserve them for future reference. Capturing this type of innovative tacit knowledge also continues to build our knowledge map and identify the innovative thinkers in the enterprise.

3. Issue Management

Once a Risk or Opportunity gets a "100%" rating it should automatically be escalated to become and Issue. Issues require resolution immediately.

The process of Issue Management is one of resolving potential or realized risks and opportunities. This is the stage where we apply all of our problem solving experience (our Tacit knowledge) to overcome obstacles and facilitate opportunities. From a knowledge management perspective, capturing the resolution thought process and capturing the nature of the proposed solution provide us with key enterprise indicators of who the experts in given areas are and the innovative thought processes used in problem resolution. This allows us to identify who can be used as a potential resource on future problems of a similar nature as well as providing us an archive of solutions.

How you resolve issues is the business of business. How we capture that process and knowledge is the business of knowledge managers.

4. Change Management

Change management is mission critical to maintaining the project Trinity. Once we've decided how to resolve an issue we need to formalize its impact to the Trinity and gain necessary approval to make the required changes in scope, timeline and budget. Who is responsible for approval and when it will take place is the responsibility of the change management process. This is less important for knowledge managers and more important to project integrity. We should capture this process and knowledge, as part of our project management framework program or log files.

The change management process itself is fairly simple. If an issue can't be resolved within a specific time frame it is escalated to the next respective change committee. Even if it is resolved it will still need to go to the respective change committee for proper approval and sign-off.

You typically have three change committees:

Tier 1-Change Committee

Who: Usually the project team leaders

Authority: Can authorize changes in scope that don't affect timeline or budget.

Tier 2-Change Committee

Who: Usually the project sponsor and project manager

Authority: Can authorize changes in scope and timeline that doesn't affect the budget.

Tier 3-Change Committee

Who: Usually the Board of Directors or Governance Board

Authority: Can authorize changes in scope, timeline or budget.

Each committee is assigned a specific response turn around time. If they fail to respond, then the issue is escalated. This also helps break political barriers that often develop during projects when two different departments or people have different objectives in mind.

Proxy Reporting

We've now covered the Trinity and Management controls which takes us to Proxy reporting as the third topic in project management.

Before I describe proxy reporting I'll describe the process of initializing a project.

Prior to commencement of any project there is always a proposal. The proposal usually states the vision of the project, its anticipated costs and the intended benefits. This is usually fairly conceptual and high-level, creating a broad-stroke perspective. Once we've drafted the proposal we need to find a sponsor. The sponsor is the person who will take the idea to the Board of directors and get approval and funding. The Board is not going to release all the funding required because this is just a concept at this stage and the total funding model hasn't been developed anyway. They are likely to approve only a limited amount of funds and time to complete the next stage of the project, the Feasibility Study.

It's at the feasibility study phase that we begin to engage the project framework. Usually we perform the feasibility in somewhat of an isolated mode that avoids disrupting the enterprise with communications about something that may not even happen. We take our most educated guesses about corporate impact and test them against what we know on a localized basis. There is usually a very limited time allocated to the feasibility and often this step may be outsourced to a third party to offer an objective perspective.

Regardless of who develops the feasibility, the result is delivered to the Project Sponsor who, in turn, delivers it to the Board. Should the Board agree with the feasibility they will then typically release funding for the next phase that we will call the Detailed Analysis Phase. At this stage the feasibility becomes a project. Now that we have a project we register it and assign it a project number. This is where the framework kicks in.

The Key to Successful Proxy Reporting:

*"In order for a project management framework to work, the fundamental components of the framework **MUST** become part of the base job descriptions of **everyone** in the enterprise."*

Most importantly, the management across the organization must have a simple process integrated into their daily job function that makes it **mandatory** they participate in the project communication system.

As part of the management job description they must be notified of, and review, any potential project that can affect their respective areas. Therefore, when the project is registered it is the responsibility of the Project Sponsor to formally advertise the existence of this new project and disseminate the required reading (the feasibility study at this point) to the rest of the management team within a specified time frame.

After they receive the feasibility study, it then becomes the mandated responsibility of the management team to review and respond to the Project Sponsor any risks, opportunities or issues they have or foresee with the project, within a specified time frame.

Here's where the proxy kicks in. *"There must be an organizationally mandated rule that anyone not responding within the allotted time frames will be proxied."* That's it! It's that simple. Too often politics are the reason so many projects fall prey to failure, over-runs or never get started. Proxy reporting circumvents the politics of delay and keeps the project timelines in sync.

As the project moves through its allotted phases, as each meeting takes place in the organization, as each decision is faced and multiple people need to be involved, Proxy reporting keeps the wheels of time commitment moving. You can use this for everything in your enterprise that needs to be agreed to in groups large or small when issues need to be resolved. Proxy reporting works! I use it in everything I do when managing projects. There is nothing like seeing the expression on someone's face when you tell him or her you made a decision on his or her behalf. You can bet they'll show up for the next meeting and the one after that.

Of course the one caveat is *that the Board of Directors must mandate this as part of peoples base job descriptions.* There will likely be contracts in place between the organization and the management staff. If you try to invoke this without top-level commitment it will fail.

The following illustrations represent the order of communications.

Step 1: The Board mandates the Project Management Framework to all staff

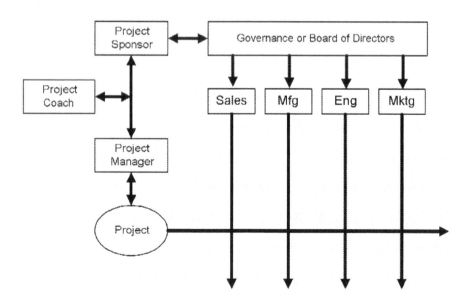

Step 2: The project is registered and notification sent out

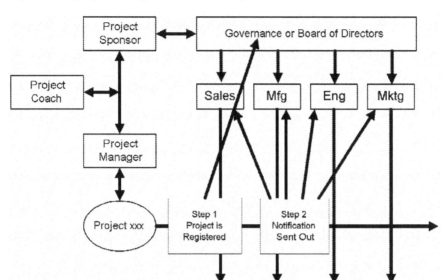

Step 3: Feedback is required in specific time frame or participants are proxied.

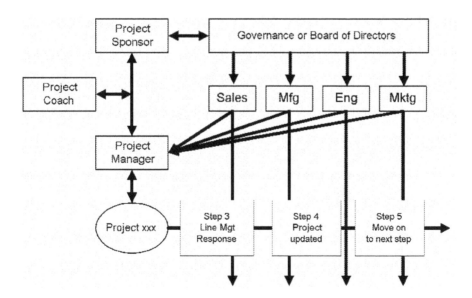

Post Implementation Review

The final component of the Project Management Framework is the Post Implementation Review or the "PIR" for short. The PIR is very important to the knowledge management effort because of its purpose within the project itself.

The purpose of the PIR is to get the project participants together at the end of the project to sit down and digest the project as a whole. It is during this stage that we analyze all the things that went wrong and all the things we did right. We document our problems in general and contemplate innovative ways to avoid these sorts of troubles in the future. We also document all the practices that proved most successful and contemplate ways to communicate these practices to other projects and people.

"The ability to capitalize on our successes, large and small, is the fundamental key to our survival."

The PIR takes place after the project is finished and therefore can't influence the project at all. What the PIR can do is capture the lessons learned into a formal knowledge management system so others can participate in the findings and experiences. This step is all too frequently avoided as it takes time, and most people have long since moved on to bigger and better things. It's important that project managers don't release project team members from this phase of the project responsibilities until the results are well documented and transferred into the knowledge base.

How and When to Measure

The importance of measurement is dependent upon which phase of your KM Program you are in. The following graph is representative of measurement importance in relation to program phase:

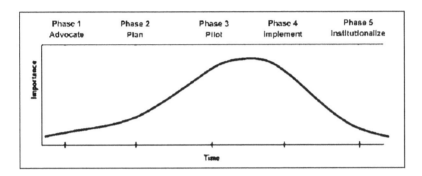

Measurements per Phase

KM – Measurements Phase 1

Advocate

- Time of Advocacy
- No Measurements Required
- Do NOT Measure Financial here

KM – Measurements Phase 2

Plan

1. **Measure for Progress in Phase 1**
   (Sponsors, Presentations to Key Players, Money Raised)

2. **Measure the Gap**
   (Where are we, Where do we want to be, Gap Analysis)

3. **Measure against Benchmarks**
   (What are others like us doing and how well)

4. **Measure Cultural Readiness**
   (Where do we share today. Is credit given where credit is due)

5. **Do NOT Measure Financial here**

KM – Measurements Phase 3

Pilot

1. Business Value (Measure Financial Here)
   (Clock Speed = Labor Costs)
   Ancillary - (Redistribution of People, Time to Market,
   Support Staff Reductions)
2. Knowledge Usage (are they coming back for more)
3. Cultural Impact (are they buying, selling and brokering)
4. Effectiveness of Sharing Communities
5. Cost of Capture and Compilation vs. Value
6. Cost Analysis of Pilot Project
7. Lessons Learned become Metrics for Next Pilot

KM – Measurements Phase 4

Implement

1. Community & Marketplace

- Knowledge volumes into and out of communities

- Amount of feedback coming into and out of communities

- Quality of feedback

2. Level of KM integration into Workflow

KM – Measurements Phase 5

Institutionalize

1. Integration of KM into Business Model

2. Integration of KM into Performance Evaluations

The measurements section is contributed by the America Productivity & Quality Center (APQC–www.apqc.org). I use these measurements as a good guideline for KM measurement. I've modified the phase names to suit my needs.

Measuring knowledge management (KM) is not simple. Determining KM's pervasiveness and impact is analogous to measuring the contribution of marketing, employee development, or any other management or organizational competency. It is nonetheless a necessity if KM is to last and have significant impact in an organization.

During its 2000 consortium learning forum entitled Successfully Implementing Knowledge Management, APQC focused on how some of the most advanced early KM adopters implement a knowledge management initiative, mobilize resources, create a business case, and measure and evolve their KM programs. This multi-client benchmarking project helped APQC and project participants identify measurement approaches, specific measures in use, and how measures impact and are impacted by the evolution of KM.

The following graph emerged from observing the numerous organizations that participated in the project—those sponsoring the consortium learning forum (sponsor organizations) and those identified as having best-practice processes in place (partner organizations)—and how they measure the value of knowledge management. In the earliest stages of knowledge management implementation, formal measurement rarely takes place, nor is it required. As KM becomes more structured and widespread and companies move into Stages two, three, and four, the need for measurement steadily increases. As KM becomes institutionalized—a way of doing business—the importance of KM-specific measures diminishes, and the need to measure the effectiveness of knowledge-intensive business processes replaces them.

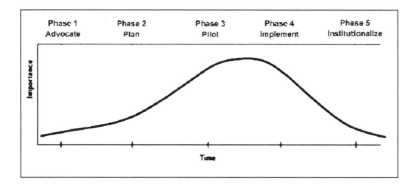

APQC collaborated with Corning, Dow Corning, and Siemens AG to find real-world examples of measures throughout the stages and gain perspective on how organizations deal with the perennial question, "How do we measure the value of KM?"

STAGE 1: ADVOCATE

The fire to manage knowledge starts with the spark of inspiration. There has to be a new source of energy or interest to cause KM to appear in the option set for the organization. Someone must become inspired with the vision of what it would be like if the organization could effectively support human knowledge capture, transfer, and use. Energized by his or her vision, this champion begins to search for opportunities to share the vision with others and to find opportunities to demonstrate the value of KM to the organization. The central task for the champion at this stage is to create a vision that inspires others to join in the exploration of how managing knowledge might contribute value to the enterprise and its people.

Measures Appropriate for Stage 1

The value of embarking on the KM journey needs to be understood by management—more in theory at this stage than in quantitative numbers. The most effective way of convincing them may be to find the greatest areas of "pain" within your organization. Find redundant efforts, discover areas where knowledge is lost, and find points of frustration in your employee base. It is important to expose the need for knowledge management at this stage.

Interviewing key stakeholders helps uncover KM needs and exposes areas of lost time, effort, and therefore money. Making comparisons with similar industries that have successfully implemented KM also can convince skeptics. If your competitor has gained recognition for its KM efforts and has seen its productivity jump and operating costs plummet, you have likely found a good candidate to use as proof of KM's power.

Stage 1 is the time for advocating the potential of KM. Once you have others on board, more concrete measures will be necessary.

STAGE 2: PLAN

During the second stage of KM implementation a practical definition of knowledge management is formulated within an organization and consideration of its applicability is made. The movement can start from several isolated, grassroots knowledge-enabling activities and develop into a cross-corporate vision and strategy. The development of several successful knowledge-enabling practices and pilots can be the catalyst to draw positive senior management attention. Further, it allows organizational sponsors to realize and consequently support the formation of a cross-functional team that can bring alignment.

At this point in the process, negotiations for some corporate funding can add additional resources to the scarce and limited funds from the local teams. Toward the end of this stage, the pilots' focus begins to center on specific knowledge management ideas and principles in order to demonstrate concepts and capabilities.

Measures Appropriate for Stage 2

We begin to see the emergence of a need for measurement in Stage 2 as interest about KM escalates in several parts of the organization. These measures can appear in three main categories: anecdotal (war stories, success stories, etc.), quantitative (growth), and qualitative (mainly extrapolation from anecdotal). It is appropriate to begin this section by identifying what should not be measured in Stage 2. Since most management initiatives are driven by financial results, the instinct is to identify quantifiable financial measurements such as productivity increases, increased sales, reduced overhead, etc.

Knowledge management will generate these financial measurements and others but not in the early stages. Measurement of financial returns or results should not be undertaken at this point except as byproducts of other concurrent efforts. *Simply stated, if you are measuring for financial returns when your organization is at this particular juncture, then you are measuring the wrong thing.*

Focus should be on meaningful measures that concentrate on exploring the various opportunities in your organization for implementing knowledge management practices, developing your organization's knowledge management strategies, measuring the progress toward organizational awareness, and experimenting with different knowledge management concepts. You should concentrate on developing and selling the concept and then measure against your plan.

Examples of Stage 2 Measures

Simple measures are critical at this stage. Examples of potential measurements include:

Measure for Progress

Measure the progress you make in developing and growing sponsorship and support. How successful are you in gaining senior management's attention, e.g., is anyone listening to you? Measurement here is largely anecdotal with some quantitative measurements such as:

> ➤ the number of sponsors you can recruit both as champions and as project sponsors,

> ➤ how many times you can get in front of decision makers to make presentations and the responses you receive, and

> ➤ how much corporate underwriting and other funding you can get. If all you receive is verbal support and no time or money, your measurement of results should indicate a need to rethink your strategy.

Measure the Gap

As part of your early work in Stages 1 and 2, you should have completed an assessment or knowledge map of your organization to determine what practices you currently have in place and what you are missing. As part of this assessment, you should attempt to identify what, if any, measurements are currently being used. You will at some point need to determine the value of that measurement and whether it can be used going forward. The existing measurement can at a minimum provide you a benchmark for future measurements.

Measure Against a Benchmark

Benchmarking with other organizations can be a persuasive tool and can lead to executive sponsorship. Since most successful KM initiatives are grassroots or organizational (department/division) and not corporate (top-down) in origin, measuring where you are in developing your program against other parts of the company can be useful. How many organizations have KM initiatives under way? What is their funding, staffing, and reporting structure? These types of measures can help you promote your KM program to your management.

If your top managers perceive that enabling knowledge capture and transfer is receiving attention in other organizations, they may be inclined to support you. If your KM activities can be shown to be less advanced than others', management may gain incentive to provide additional focus and resources. If you are out in front of the other organizations, management may increase support to maintain the perception of leadership, which may also help you develop contacts for tacit knowledge sharing.

A company routinely captures its research intellectual property in the form of formal reports that are stored in the library. The library measures the volume of reports turned in by each department and forwards the numbers to department management, which can then use the numbers to determine the per capita reports being generated and other measurements. The number of reports accessed on an annual basis and specific areas of interest are also measured.

One approach may be to understand what your competitors or other government sectors are doing in leveraging knowledge sharing for their customers and within their organizations. Gaining an understanding of what your suppliers, customers, and peer organizations are doing to enable knowledge sharing within their organizations and externally may also be a good idea.

Measure Your Cultural Readiness

It is important at this stage to build the foundation to develop a knowledge-sharing culture. Critical practices that foster employee information exchange, teamwork, collaboration, and trust development can be built upon through crediting the contributors. Look for teams that operate in this manner. Begin to collect the team's social norms and practices and determine if insights can be incorporated into other teams. Document stories to encourage role model behavior.

STAGE 3: PILOT

This stage signals the formal implementation of a knowledge management initiative. The goal of Stage 3 is to provide evidence of knowledge management's business value by conducting pilots and capturing lessons learned that can be transferred and used to help the organization better implement KM on a larger and expanding scale.

The framework for communities of practice begins to be formalized at this stage, and funding and support is derived from a mix of central resources as well as the donation of time, people, and money from within organizations that are enthusiastic about enabling knowledge sharing.

Measures Appropriate for Stage 3

There is a convergence at Stage 3 of the three main categories of measurement that exist in the early stages of KM implementation stages: anecdotal, quantitative, and qualitative. The degree of rigor and refinement becomes more defined and focused on business strategy in Stage 3. The key here is to begin to ensure that direct business value is perceived by the organization as a result of the knowledge-enabling projects. It is important to establish a mechanism to capture the hard and soft lessons learned in the knowledge management pilots, as these will be the building blocks for the later KM stages.

Having a predefined taxonomy on the classification of lessons learned can be helpful in developing conclusions and identifying areas desirable for replication throughout an organization. In addition, during the acceleration of knowledge management scale-up, establishing measures for the various components of a knowledge management initiative is beneficial. These measures include process dimensions, culture dimensions, content dimensions, information technology dimensions, and people dimensions.

Examples of Stage 3 Measures

Measure the Business Value

Document both the hard and soft business value derived from each pilot. Begin to map measurements to your specific business goals such as improved clock speed. This does not necessarily need to be rigorous at this point. Extrapolation of anecdotal measurements into more solid quantifiable measurements occurs. Can the pilot results be duplicated in other parts of the organization?

Time saved equals direct labor cost, which is easy to figure. Effort needs to be put into determining the ancillary costs associated with time savings. Some potential areas are resource redistribution, support staff cost reductions, and improved time to market.

Measure the Retention of Knowledge

Measure the amount of information contributed to the knowledge base over time against the retrieval and reuse. Quantifiable measurements are not enough; they must be balanced with qualitative data to ensure an accurate, full picture. Unlike in previous stages, the number of hits on a Web site is not good enough. Specific measures and issues to be considered may include the following:

➤ Time spent per hit. This can reveal if individuals entering the site are actually reviewing its content (indicates quick review and rejection vs. what would constitute an individual actually digesting some content). This would have to be correlated with the number of individuals using it for an extended period of time and repeat users.

➤ Are the IP addresses those of repeat users? The intent for this measurement is to track repeat customers somehow. Repeat customers indicate two things—either specific information is of repeatable use to them or they find value in the additional information continually added to the application.

➤ How often is a site visited?

➤ What percentage of total hits represent repeat users? Value can be measured by repeat business.

➤ What is the threshold for indicating a repeat user is a steady customer? Someone may sample a site several times, but will stop visiting if they fail to get the results they seek.

Measure the Cultural Impact

In Stage 3, the issues surrounding the potential for measuring the cultural side of knowledge management need to be addressed. Considerable effort needs to placed on determining:

➤ the types of measurements,

➤ the potential value of the measurements,

➤ the cost for measuring vs. the value of measuring, and

➤ processes.

In selecting measures, consideration should be given to if and how the cultural side (the big side) of KM can be measured in Stage 3.
Anecdotal stories. How do we measure it? As stated earlier, stories can form the basis for extrapolation of quantitative data. This is not necessarily the only or best means of using anecdotal measurements, but considering the intrinsic value of the anecdote can be important. Can a story or a lesson learned have behavioral impact that cannot be measured directly or in traditional terms?

Performance review. Another means of measuring cultural impact is through the performance review process. Individuals can be rated by their peers (360-degree feedback) on three major knowledge-sharing points listed below. This can be implemented in Stage 3 because there are formal (if only pilot) applications in place. As part of these applications, feedback on the usefulness of the knowledge provided is essential.

> Do they share their knowledge in an open and constructive way?

> Do others find their knowledge of value and use it? What results are gained from it? This can also be demonstrated through venting processes for inclusion in databases and use of that information.

> Do they use others' knowledge and apply it to improve operations? This can be measured somewhat by traditional business measurement tools.

Public and private recognition and rewards for individuals and teams. Though we advocate team building and sharing of knowledge, incentives for individual contributions are still required. A reward or recognition system properly implemented can provide quantitative measurements.

Measure the Effectiveness of Sharing Communities

Document the effectiveness of communities of practices (CoPs). Based on findings, determine essential elements that contribute to a coherent and effective CoP. Draw correlations against CoPs that have not been as successful. Extract lessons learned and best practices from these correlations and use them to build new CoPs and improve existing ones.

Measure the Ownership of Capture and Compilation

What are the costs involved in capturing information in a usable manor? This includes not only the capturing but also the indexing. If the information is not retrievable, it is of little value. Quantifiable measurement of the time required to capture the information in a usable manner is applicable. This can be critical in evaluating the impact of a pilot project. Is the cost of the capture process too expensive in comparison to the value of the captured information or knowledge?

Consider story telling as an example. Here are some of the factors to be considered.

> Creating the storytelling environment (either electronic production or live storytelling)

> If live, what is the time commitment of participants (storyteller and audience)?

> If electronic, what are the production costs?

> Are the storage and distribution costs insignificant?

> How much responsibility is there on the individual to capture his information in a usable manor? This includes not only the capturing but also the indexing. If the information is not retrievable, it is of little value.

> Does the measurement of capture and compilation warrant effort?

Measure Project Management Effectiveness and Intended Results

Successful pilots will contribute to building organizational support and future funding. To ensure that projects are managed effectively, it is beneficial to track the projects. Was a formal methodology employed? Was a time line established and progress tracked? Were project objectives and expectations clearly stated and measured? Measure the performance of the pilots themselves against the intended results or hypothesis. Measurements can be quantitative, qualitative, or anecdotal.

Measuring cost in your pilots can provide critical information for determining program direction and strategy. If properly set up, measurements can enable a KM team to rethink its priorities in an efficient and timely manner, allowing for shifting resources to strengthen the potential for success.

Can the capturing of lessons learned from your pilots be used for measurements? The obvious answer is yes.

An organization can quantify these in two basic ways: number submitted and number referenced.

A qualitative measurement can be reached through a feedback measurement system such as Xerox—Eureka's thumbs up or down method of capturing the value of a tip to a user. Other measurements can be made using the number of times a lesson was used or through a feedback system allowing the capture of users' comments.

STAGE 4: IMPLEMENT

When an organization reaches Stage 4, KM has proved valuable enough to be officially expanded to become part of the organization's funded activities. Demand for KM support by other parts of the organization tends to be high, providing additional evidence of its value. Pilot results are an added benefit.

High visibility and the authority to expand are a mixed blessing; the added visibility of costs and resources devoted to KM will require more formal business evaluation and ROI justification. The good news is that unless unforeseen factors derail the efforts, KM is on its way to being considered a strategic and necessary competency.

Measures Appropriate for Stage 4

Since organizations at Stage 4 are undertaking multiple projects in diverse areas of the business, it becomes necessary to evaluate the fitness of the knowledge areas in relation to the whole organization. Evaluating a knowledge area project might require examining many areas of fitness that, in aggregate, help the organization determine whether the projects in its KM portfolio are of high impact and beneficial to the success of the company.

Project criteria may include:

Proficiency. Has a process become world-class because of KM, or has it made only mediocre improvement?

Diffusion. Has KM been properly executed? Is the Program and knowledge managed well? Is it well understood?

Codification. Because codifying knowledge is expensive, should the organization limit that? Is that limitation visible and understood?

Openness for combination/innovation. Is the knowledge described in jargon that no one understands? Is the knowledge-base open to other disciplines? Does the project generate questions to the organization to help it grow?

Justification measures can be difficult when the organization is trying to decide whether to adopt KM as part of the ongoing corporate strategy. The question of measurement must often be restated at this stage. The organization has to not only measure how knowledge area projects perform but also evaluate how it feels the business key indicators are linked to the knowledge areas. This can be easier if the business owner decides what needs to be improved through a project before embarking on it. When the improvements occur, he or she can communicate the causal linkages between where the business started and where it ended up because of the concentration on creating a viable knowledge project.

At this stage, it is important to tap into the values of the organization and determine whether a culture shift is occurring. Personal performance reviews can be a useful avenue to determine whether managers support knowledge sharing and give employees a chance to show their ability to share. Then questions can be asked of employees to determine whether management really does support knowledge sharing. Targeted questions such as "How do you support creation and innovation?" can also help determine employee mind-set.

Although most corporate KM programs have been well-established and "proven" by Stage 4, it is still important to show that KM is working and will work going forward. To estimate ROI, add the costs of a community (including labor, meetings, facilities) and then define how much effort is spent on KM by knowledge management experts. Then decide how much effort has been saved by sharing solutions in the community.

Another way to approach ROI estimation might be by looking at sub-communities and their generation of solutions in terms of community projects. If a group needs a solution and embarks on a knowledge-creation effort, determine how much has been saved in time to market, competitive positioning, etc.

Examples of Stage 4 Measures

To help prove the value of KM in its organization, Siemens is currently making a master plan of KM metrics that contains measures for each of four dimensions of its holistic KM system:

- ➤ Knowledge community: the organization, community, people dimensions

- ➤ Knowledge marketplace: the technology involved

- ➤ Key KM processes: the sharing and creation that takes place

- ➤ Knowledge environment: encompasses the above

Community and Marketplace

Thinking in those terms, Siemens has realized that it can easily evaluate the success of its communities and marketplaces with such measures as:

- ➤ how much knowledge comes into or out of the community,

- ➤ the amount of feedback that comes into and out of the community, and

- ➤ the quality of feedback.

Since Siemens believes communities are the heart of the KM system, it has spent a great deal of time on CoP assessments-questionnaires for community members that provide ideas on how to improve the community and what the impact of the community has been on someone's business.

Environment

In addition, a company can measure its knowledge environment through sophisticated methods of value assessment, i.e., measuring the values of employees and business owners to see if they match. To determine the values, an outside firm asks a series of questions to determine the level of importance various issues register with people. For example, a question might be "Is it more important for you to exchange experiences with friends or create something new in your environment?"

The results of this effort have led the company to incorporate several new principles into the corporate value system.

KM Processes

Siemens has tried to check the health of processes to determine the performance of the sharing process. Ideally, the measures would evaluate whether a person has managed the process correctly and set the right limits on it. This would give Siemens a good way to not only look at the marketplace but also examine how much sharing and creation is taking place.

As a Whole

To monitor the entire KM system, it is possible to perform a KM maturity assessment that defines whether the process is still ad hoc and chaotic or has progressed to an optimized state, for example. Siemens measures its four dimensions and 16 enablers, each of which has a set of questions. With a diagram showing the maturity for each dimension, an organization can get a feel for its maturity level.

Measures appropriate at Stage 4 are carried out with the future in mind. The value of KM principles has already been proven and companies in this stage are focused on how to embed KM throughout their organizations. Measures are used at this stage not to prove, but rather to improve, the existing projects and add to the corporate-wide strategy.

STAGE 5: INSTITUTIONALIZE

In some ways, Stage 5 is the continuation of Stage 4 to its logical conclusion of full enterprise-wide deployment. However, Stage 5 differs from Stage 4 in three fundamental ways:

> ➢ It does not happen unless KM is embedded in the business model. The organization structure must be realigned.

> ➢ Evidence of knowledge management competency becomes part of the formal performance evaluation.

> ➢ Sharing and using knowledge become part of the organization's "way of doing business" as well as an expected management competency. In the relatively young arena of KM, only a few organizations have reached this stage.

As in Stage 4, Stage 5 measures are not used to prove value. They are used to check progress and monitor the continued evolution of the culture. KM can no longer be called an initiative or project at this stage: Your organization relies on it.

Contributing authors on this section were: Cynthia Hartz of Dow Corning, Stuart Sammis of Corning, Dr. Josef Hofer-Alfeis of Siemens AG, Kimberly Lopez of APQC, Cynthia Raybourn of APQC, and Jennifer Neumann Wilson of APQC.

Why KM Programs Fail

The survey results speak for themselves.

KM Programs that Failed

The Survey Says!

Most Citied Reasons:

20% - Lack of user uptake owing to lack of communication

19% - Failure to integrate KM into everyday workflow processes

18% - Lack of time to learn / too complicated

15% - Lack of training

13% - Users could not see personal benefits

7% - Senior Management was not behind it

7% - Unsuccessful due to technical problems

(KPMG Survey)

KM Maturity Test

1. Analyze which aspects you currently implement.

People	Process
• Implementing KM awareness • Appointing Knowledge Officers • Building KM Definitions • Rewarding knowledge working • Building communities of practice • Building formal KM Networks	• Benchmarking Current KM • Creating KM Strategy • Implementing Processes for Communities of Practice • Designing other KM processes • Carrying out KM Assessment
Content	**Technology**
• Measuring Intellectual Capital • Creating Taxonomies • Defining Best Practices • Implementing Knowledge Policies	• Capturing Best Practices • Using Collaboration Software • Identifying Subject Matter Experts • Providing a Questions Matrix

2. Figure out where you are.

Level 1 – Knowledge Chaotic (3 or less)

Level 2 – Knowledge Aware (4 or more from at least 2 sections)

Level 3 – Knowledge Focused (6 or more from at least 3 sections)

Level 4 – Knowledge Managed (more than 2 from each section)

Level 5 – Knowledge Centric (All)

Step 1–Performing a KM Assessment

The road to success begins with the first step. In this section we will outline the necessary steps to follow to begin collecting the information required before building a knowledge management program.

Step 1 – Establish the definition of KM

Step 1-When starting your research efforts the first step is to define knowledge management. It is imperative that everyone concerned with the knowledge management effort has a common definition and vocabulary to provide a solid foundation for discourse. The most logical way to proceed would be to buy many additional copies of this book. Pass them out to everyone. Yes, I believe your dog needs one to.

Step 2 – Define the logical and physical structures

Step 2-You will need to map out the physical organization of the enterprise. Geographies play a major part in collaboration and knowledge transfer. Geography influences both Tacit and Explicit knowledge efforts as it affects awareness and access of knowledge resources as well as requirements for communication infrastructure.

Next we work on gathering the logical structure of the enterprise. The logical structure is the departmentalization or categorization of the organization and could potentially become the foundation for an initial taxonomy.

It is relevant to also collect the perceived utopian logical model, as there may be a hidden or expressed desire to re-engineer the logical model.

You must also collect the rationale behind any potential re-engineering efforts to get a better grasp of current perceived inefficiencies in the corporate structure.

Step 3 – Define existing corporate reporting

Step 3–You need to ascertain the existing corporate reporting structure, as these are the existing "hard coded" methods of communication and dissemination. These may play a significant or minor part in the knowledge flow through an enterprise but the use of titles is often accredited with the identification of specific repositories of knowledge. There may be no validity to the claim that someone is knowledgeable about what is described in their title or in their willingness to participate in knowledge transfer but at this stage you take nothing for granted.

Step 4 – Determine perceived KM problems

Step 4–It is crucial at this juncture that the topmost officials in the organization define for you what they perceive are the inefficiencies in knowledge management in their organization. This information is critical to the formulation of the Vision Statement.

This is where you will define your metrics for success "prior" to commencing your KM initiative. Knowledge management has gained a reputation for being "touchy feely" and not concrete. This is where we change that. You can choose a very clear and precise measuring stick at this point upon which to base the impact of KM process implementation. Pick a problem and go solve it. It's really much easier fighting a battle if you know who the enemy is.

These problems will be the motivators, both financially and organizationally for any KM project. This is also where you will find your funding. The knowledge management effort must be bound back to and measured against the problems it is intended to rectify. Throughout the life of this project you will always be returning to the vision statement to test yourself and the nature of your deliverables.

Any deviation from the vision statement must be forwarded to the knowledge management steering committee or whatever governance body is established; through proper change management initiatives that are in place, to maintain the scope of the KM project.

Step 5 – Determine the perceived utopian KM model

Step 5—You must now ascertain, from the senior most officials, what they perceive is the utopian knowledge management environment for the enterprise. Do not limit this discussion to the specific scope of this particular KM initiative, you will need a broad sweeping picture of the long term goals of the enterprise and their impressions of knowledge management in general to make sure that your initiative is in synchronization with the long-term vision.

You will eventually need to drill down to specifics about this particular project to define the scope, timeline and budget (the Trinity of project management). This effort should take into account any efforts the organization is making now or planned for the future for internal, external and inter-organizational knowledge transfer. It is also relevant at this stage to ascertain whether or not there are particular components of the internal organization or entities outside the organization with whom they intend to merge, separate, sell or acquire in the near future.

Step 6 – Determine the existing project framework

Step 6–It is important in this step to determine if they have an enterprise model for project management. A project management framework will be providing their organization with an enterprise scale knowledge delivery mechanism that can be capitalized on for not only deploying this particular KM venture but as a wealth of knowledge resources, knowledge flow patterns and existing communities of practice.

Project management is specifically designed to offer structure to knowledge and structure to reporting mechanisms, which will encompass risk, opportunity, issue and change management. These functions of project management are significant repositories of Tacit knowledge. The project document stores are excellent repositories of Explicit knowledge and best practices. Finally, if the project management framework exists, it is an excellent, if not mandatory, vehicle for deploying your own KM initiative.

Step 7 – Determine in-house KM technologies

Step 7–Determine what, if any, knowledge management specific technologies are in use at the moment or projected. Significant historical research in tools for KM is usual in most organizations because it is the most widely publicized component of knowledge management.

The organization may also have already undertaken knowledge management initiatives in the past and may have failed or are currently using some methodology that they deem relevant to your current effort. If they have tried in the past and failed it is wise to expose the history at this stage and attempt to determine why the historic KM project failed or didn't produce the anticipated results. This information may provide valuable clues for successful completion of your current KM project.

> *Step 8 – Determine current communications systems ructure*

Step 8–Due diligence is required on the entire communication infrastructure from LAN's, WAN's and MAN,s to protocols and technologies. In the instance where the KM project is focused on Tacit knowledge, bandwidth between participants becomes the single most significant factor. As I stated earlier, Tacit knowledge is best transferred face-to-face, providing the mechanisms for knowledge brokering and generating a trust level unattainable in text-based communications.

Tacit KM solutions will almost invariably wind up taking full advantage of communication technology focused on video conferencing and collaboration. These applications are very bandwidth consumptive and require robust network infrastructure and careful bandwidth planning.

Frequently, the IT section of an organization is delegated the responsibility to deliver KM projects, and the IT section almost invariably has nothing to do with the telecommunications section. Delivery mechanisms for Tacit KM should account for all communication mediums including the organizations telephone system(s) that are often designed from the ground up to handle video conferencing demands.

The delivery of audio, video and data communications could include broadband transmission (Cable Television infrastructure), microwave, satellite or other wireless technologies. All of these technologies must be considered as viable communication mediums with substantial differences in delivery costs and functionality.

Step 9 – Determine workstation configurations

Step 9–Here we identify the desktop productivity tools currently in use, identifying the type and versions prevalent throughout the enterprise. We also want to establish the lowest common denominator of workstations and the current configurations (how much RAM on machines, hard drive capacities, CPU speeds, level of graphics. etc.).

Delivery of desktop components is the single most time consuming aspect of deployment. Knowledge management technologies for desktops (especially desktop video conferencing) can be very machine consumptive. Machines and desktop productivity tools may also present myriad operating systems and delivery applications as well as multiple versions and models.

Standardization of desktop machines to participate in KM would be nice but not always within budget, timeline or feasibility if machines are deployed around specific mission-critical business application requirements. This information is crucial to determine the true cost of deployment, as **this is typically the most expensive aspect of deployment.**

Modifying user workstations also has dramatic effect on visual impact to the user community and the need for additional end-user training. Mobile users present problems of their own as they are typically limited in available bandwidth and by security concerns, all of which must be calculated into the risk analysis and funding model for the project.

Step 10 – Determine current messaging platforms

Step 10–Determine the nature and extent of existing messaging platforms. Messaging platforms include both the traditional e-mail systems as well as application messaging systems (such as Microsoft's MSMQ or similar). Messaging systems play an important role in knowledge management as they provide an efficient form of alternate asynchronous communication, which is conducive to workflow integration of knowledge management technologies.

Messaging in the form of e-mail is a cornerstone in today's communication infrastructure but provides two significant barriers in knowledge management.

The first problem with e-mail is that it provides little or no opportunity to facilitate the brokering of knowledge. Once someone has documented a piece of valuable knowledge then, once transmitted, is available for public broadcast and dissemination. Once knowledge is passed on it is perceived to diminish in value to the originator and therefore offers a psychological roadblock to knowledge transfer.

The second problem with e-mail is that people rarely desire to broadcast that they don't know something. Once a piece of knowledge is documented and broadcast it is now Explicit and can and should be continually challenged to provide further validation. People don't typically enjoy being proven wrong and therefore are frequently reluctant to pass along a piece of interpolative information, which is at the heart of Tacit or innovative knowledge.

Step 11 – Determine types of data storage systems

Step 11–In this step we attempt to understand and locate information repositories and existing applications that can provide the information framework and tools to support our KM undertaking.

Data repositories mainly consist of:

- PIM Software
- Groupware / Collaboration Software
- Databases of any type
- Web Servers / File Servers
- Content / Document Management
- Data Warehouse / Data Mining Software
- HR and Accounting Systems
- Artificial Intelligence Systems
- ERP Software
- Business Process Automation Software
- Search Software
- Communities of Practice
- Portals, Registries, Directory Services
- Taxonomies, Meta-Data, Maps
- Question Relationship Matrices
- SME Identification Software / Systems

Step 12 – Determine location of repositories

Step 12–After identifying the types of data repositories we need to now identify the physical location of the repositories.

This process usually consists of identifying the physical location, make, model and configurations of servers. It is a good idea to identify the network segments and available bandwidth into each device as KM tools can often significantly load and tax existing network and server infrastructure.

Eventually we will need to estimate the potential demands that will be placed on each device and determine if network or system upgrades are required to facilitate the KM demands.

Step 13 – Determine current security model

Step 13–Security concerns are or should be prevalent in any information system and communication network. Considering that we are dealing with one of the most significant aspects in any organization (intellectual capital) we must articulate that security should be even more significant an effort in this situation.

A careful review of the existing security policies, processes and methodology is required at this stage. At this point we are not debating security but simply collecting the information with regards to the existing security model.

Step 14 – Determine requirements for P & M

Step 14–This step is the determination of the organizations need for personalization and membership.

The importance of personalization and membership is amplified by the discussions on taxonomies. Users classify information differently than organizations because they have different objectives. Users are trying to navigate the Frid Decision Cycle and codify information and relationships in order to solve a problem. The information and relationships are usually dynamic and ephemeral. Codification at the organization level, on the other hand, is usually fairly static and viewed from the organizational perspective.

Therefore we need both organizational and personal methods of classifying, categorizing and indexing. Using a multi-taxonomy approach we can expose all the taxonomies to the user communities and through personalization they can choose the best categories to utilize for their daily work requirements. In a utopian environment we would also allow users to construct their own taxonomies if we choose to implement the necessary technologies that can operate on that level of granularity.

This level of adaptation of taxonomies provides users with the ability to personalize their view into information dimensions.

Personalization and membership provides a means to make knowledge collection and transfer as personal as possible to encourage multiple audience participation.

Step 15 – Determine current directory services

Step 15–Most organizations have many directory structures. From e-mail directories to Network logon directories to corporate telephone directories. The question is not whether they have a directory; the question is more of how many directories and of what type and structure.

Consolidating directory structures is a significant and rewarding undertaking, providing a point of common data across the enterprise and providing end users and programmers with a central repository of common data.

An enterprise directory facilitates significant consolidation of programming efforts and common data input/output for everyone and every application in the organization.

Step 16 – Perform KM Survey

Step 16–The KM Survey is attached as Appendix A. The results should give you an impression of what you will be up against and where you can possibly find low hanging fruit for your first KM pilot.

Step 17 – Summarize your findings and get sign-off

Step 17–Once you have collected the research information it is now time to consolidate your findings in a document and present the current state-of-affairs to the powers that be for sign-off and approval. Pick your pilot, secure some funding and move forward into the Advocating stage.

Congratulate yourself on making it this far as you've probably turned over many stones and consumed many hours from people that all thought they are too busy to take the time you really needed.

The point is, if you didn't complete this phase of the project then there is no need to proceed to the next phase because of the near certainty of failure.

Step 2–Crafting a Vision Statement

Crafting a vision statement is critical to any projects success, not just a knowledge management project. Without a clearly articulated objective then there is little or no way to judge your direction or measure your success. "A ship afloat at sea" would be a good metaphor for those unwilling to describe, in writing, the project goals.

The more detailed we can articulate a vision statement the less room for misinterpretation. As we begin crafting we should consider the intended audience. This type of vision statement is designed as a position statement for organizational knowledge management and will have a far reaching and opinionated audience. Therefore each part of the vision should synchronize with the existing culture, the perceived future culture, the current business plan and the organizations marketing plan.

Knowledge management is a suite of pervasive support functions and is therefore a means to an end, not an end unto itself. A careful review of the organizational vision must be incorporated into the KM vision statement. This vision can be crafted by anyone with the ambition to undertake the research but the product of the statement must be acknowledged, agreed to and advertised by the Board of Directors or organization head.

A vision imposed by a sub agency, department or section could cause potential political unrest as there will be a perceived shift in power because, as Francis Bacon states "knowledge is power" and people will react according to their perceived diminished value.

I recently wrote a vision statement for a Governor in the Midwest. I started with an articulate description of our objectives so as to eliminate many days of potential debate over interpretation. I was sitting in a position of authority in one particular department of the state government. I carefully weighed the cultural and technological aspects of the different agencies and put pen to paper to craft what I thought was a well versed technological direction for statewide common intake.

I submitted the vision to the department head who immediately sliced, diced and watered down the goals. I was disappointed but could live with the resultant deliverable. From there it went to the Chief of Staff who proceeded to virtually cut it in half the "cleansed" statement and made the resulting vision so generic it could be interpreted in literally any way anyone decided. This is of course, what the Governor proceeded to water down further. By the time it was finished and submitted is was not worth the paper it was written on.

The end result was, I went before the multi-agency steering committee, with useless vision in hand and proceeded to redraft the vision verbally until I had unanimous (unbelievable for government) approval on the final vision statement that, low and behold, was vastly similar to what I started with. The problem was one we have spoken of, the level of trust. I had little prior face-to-face time with either the Chief of Staff or the Governor so I had to wait until such an opportunity could present itself that I could meet everyone involved and "sell" the vision.

It was the personal delivery of the speech and my commitment to the vision (and some substantial leg work to achieve preliminary allies) that allowed me to penetrate the hidden agendas and gain the trust necessary for execution of the vision statement. The crafting and approval process for the vision statement provided yet another excellent example to reinforce how Tacit knowledge must be brokered face-to-face to achieve results.

Keep in mind that this is an over-all Organizational KM mission statement, not a KM Program mission statement.

There is a difference. In the organizational mission statement we are driving culture. In the KM Program mission statement we are driving towards resolving a particular problem.

In a KM Program mission statement you are basically outlining a target goal and it will typically get embodied within your project charter.

With this in mind let's look at a sample *Organizational* KM Vision statement:

> *It is the goal of this organization to cultivate an environment in which its people are constantly striving for gains in both performance and innovation. What we know makes a significant contribution to the value of our enterprise and our stakeholders. The sharing of our knowledge only furthers our efforts in adding value and commitment to our mission and financial objectives.*
>
> *Knowledge should be an enabler of both performance and innovation, should better empower our people to undertake their daily tasks and provide an avenue of growth in every area or our organization.*

Our vision is to create the infrastructure necessary to facilitate the sharing of knowledge throughout the enterprise. This infrastructure will support the management of existing knowledge, the teaching and mentoring of our human resources, the reduction of redundancy and provide mechanisms to aid in person-to-person communications.

To this end it is our goal to utilize processes, methodologies, programs and technologies to deliver the necessary components that will engage the people of this organization, as well as others that participate outside our organization, in a long-term knowledge transfer strategy. In essence, our objectives are to capture into our human resource programs and technological systems both existing knowledge as well as providing the vehicles for knowledge exchange.

From a technological perspective infrastructure must be comprised of and support systems that can pull-in, push-out, index, categorize and analyze our existing knowledge. The same technology infrastructure should also facilitate face-to-face communications, provide systems that enable users to locate and qualify potential repositories of knowledge (both human and technological) and provide recognition to participants for their value-added efforts.

Participation from our staff, our partners and our customers is paramount to our success. All departments, divisions, sections and agencies must undertake to develop programs that both recognize and reward the efforts of our participants and encourage their ongoing participation, nurturing their desire to transfer their knowledge to others and strive for ever-increasing quality in the their personal knowledge gaining efforts.

Perhaps not Shakespeare, but the intent of the Vision is clear. The terminology is focused but generic enough to leave room for innovation on human resource and technological sides. A long-term vision should not emphasize specific products, programs or technologies because of the fluid nature of each. We strive not to back ourselves into corners in anything but to articulate and maintain a 50,000-foot perspective and direction.

Step 3–Defining the CKO Role

CKO verses CIO

To put it blunt terms, the Chief Knowledge Officer (CKO) is basically a proxy for the business owners and the Chief Information Officer (CIO) basically represents the technology. Of course both functions could reside within one individual or a single office, but the differentiation still exists.

Historically, we've not formally sought to split the functions consciously, although we have all split them subconsciously.

The CKO drives to stimulate innovation, whereby the CIO manages the explicit and transactional information of the business and its supporting technologies.

The goals are complimentary.

More specifically:

> **The CKO is concerned with business Decision Cycles**
> **The CIO is concerned with technology Life Cycles**

Let's look at a comparison table so you can see how each compliments the other:

CKO	CIO
Psychological	Physiological
Ownership and advocacy of organizational KM mission statement	Participates in drafting of the KM mission statement
Integrates KM into business plan	Integrates KM into IM
By utilizing the KM Decision-Cycle the CKO analyzes how knowledge is created, valued and transferred throughout the organization	By utilizing the IT Life-Cycle the CIO analyzes how information is captured, created, stored, secured, shared and destroyed.
Analyzes information provided by CIO and categorizes and classifies it by defining taxonomies and knowledge maps	Receives the taxonomies and knowledge maps from CKO and uses them to codify the information repositories
Develops meta-data standards	Binds meta-data to information
Defines Search, Filter, Relevancy, Ranking requirements	Implements Search, Filter, Relevancy, Ranking technologies
Defines questions and relevancies	Implements question matrix
Defines how to break down knowledge silos	Implements technologies that helps identify where knowledge silos exist and assist breaking them
Ensures KM is integrated in every workflow process	Implements technological KM components of workflow
Defines which and when people should work face-to-face	Implements technologies that allow face-to-face communications
Advocates the development and re-use of best practices	Facilitates the storage and retrieval of best practices
Organizes real and virtual communities of practice	Implements technologies that support communities of practice
Defines business intelligence	Implements business intelligence technologies
Identifies relevant information repositories	Manages access to relevant information repositories
Defines and implements KM incentive programs	Implements measurement technologies used in partially assessing users KM participation

I'm sure from the table above that you can begin to get the sense that, for the most part, the CKO spends most of his/her time defining things. That's because implementation is performed by the CIO for technological requirements and by Senior and Line Managers for human aspects and advocacy.

The CKO role is perpetual. Times change, people change, processes change, technologies change. For that matter, "change management" changes as well. Everything changes (except processed cheese).

The CKO is often the gatekeeper of change since the knowledge managers understand that change is actually an underlying motivator in knowledge management. At least knowledge managers are ensured gainful employment until computers become sentient.

Now that we know what a Chief Knowledge Officer is let's better define the CKO role.

Sample Role and Responsibilities:

Scope

This policy establishes the minimum administrative responsibilities for the agency appointed Chief Knowledge Officer (CKO). This policy must be reviewed frequently to reflect changes in people, processes and technology.

Community

Intended Audience-This document is intended for Agency Management Staff

Benefactors-The beneficiaries of this document will be Agency Staff

Document Owner–Your name goes here

Knowledge Management Functions

Each Division and Section of the Agency must formally recognize the responsibilities of the CKO and participate in achieving the objectives of this office. Many individuals across organizational lines may be involved as long as there is a clear separation of duties and responsibilities which provides effective checks, balances and accountability. However, it is important that one individual be designated as having primary responsibility for coordination of knowledge management objectives. It is also important that another individual be designated as a back-up CKO.

The functions to be performed by the office of the CKO shall be at a minimum:

Defining, Architecting and Documenting:

> ➤ Organizational KM Mission Statement

> ➤ Knowledge Benchmarks and Assessment Practices

> ➤ How Problems are Identified & Presented

> ➤ Relevant Questions, Relationships and Weights (Decision-Matrix)

➢ Categorization and Classification (Taxonomies, Meta-Data, Map)

➢ Knowledge Management Roles and Responsibilities

➢ How to find Information–Search, Filter, Relevancy, Ranking

➢ Rules, Thresholds & Triggers

➢ Integration of KM into Workflow Processes

➢ How to Identify and Engage Subject Matter Experts

➢ Face-to-Face Programs and Technologies

➢ Communities of Practice and Collaboration

➢ Best Practices and Knowledge Transfer Processes

➢ Context Sensitive Business Intelligence

➢ Culture Requirements (including KM Awareness Training)

➢ KM Incentive Programs

➢ Relevant Information Repositories

➢ The Value of Information

Role of an Information Security Officer

A CKO's duty is to ensure that KM policies and procedures are established and implemented to enhance and protect the intellectual capital of the Agency, participate in the creation and review of the policies and procedures, recommend KM strategies, and keep information KM programs current. The CKO has a duty to ensure that these procedures are in place.

In order to develop successful KM programs, the CKO:

- needs to understand the agency's mission, how each department and system supports that mission, how they are interconnected, and the associated and projected technologies that have been implemented;

- needs a stable resource base in terms of personnel, funds, and other support in order to plan and execute knowledge management programs and projects effectively;

- needs agency-wide cooperation to successfully implement knowledge management;

- needs to coordinate and call upon others in the agency for assistance; and

- needs to establish links to KM personnel in other parts of the organization, to other CKO's in partner agencies, and to external CKO reference sources.

Recommended: Establish an advisory board of employee advocates who represent different functions/disciplines across the organization to help develop policies and procedures and maintain continuity and stimulate participation in knowledge management programs across the organization on an ongoing basis.

The CKO's role is to:

- report to the CEO, to balance KM theories with pragmatic KM programs;

- be the agency's authority on Knowledge Management;

- recommend appropriate separation of duties and responsibilities for KM functions;

- promote KM awareness throughout the agency;

- be part of the decision-making team when the agency is developing new processes;

- be part of the decision-making team when the agency is designing, planning, procuring or upgrading technologies;

- be responsible for the development, implementation and revisions of an agency knowledge management organizational mission statement;

- be responsible for the development, implementation and revisions of an agency knowledge management policy;

- be the single point of contact for all issues involving KM including, but not limited to, questions, presentations, advocacy and measurements; and

- inform the CEO or Head of the Agency of progress, activity and risks.

Training/Education

All employees, agents and others who interact within the scope of the agency must be provided sufficient training and support to allow them to properly participate with any particular KM Program that encompasses them.

Training is an integral aspect of KM and will contribute to a learning, remembering and teaching environment. This training must encompass all users, including executive management, program, field, IT and other staff that are to be involved in any way within the scope of a KM Program. Trained users will be better participants and will likely be more proactive in helping others as well as encouraging additional participants.

The CKO should also keep current on all areas of knowledge management including, but not limited to new KM technologies, KM literature, theories, best practices and new techniques. Therefore, the CKO should receive KM and appropriate business and technical training on a regular basis.

The CKO's role is to:

- identify appropriate KM training for agency staff including, but not limited to, the KM mission statement and KM policies;

- stay current via training and publications about KM issues;

- review all upcoming technological projects with the CIO;

- review all upcoming business projects with the Line Management;

- receive regular update training on KM; and

- review publications and other information regarding KM.

Agency Knowledge Management Policy

A key portion of the CKO's role is to develop and implement an agency-specific knowledge management policy in concert with the appropriate executive staff. The executive staff should include, but not be limited to, Board of Directors or Ministers, Deputy Ministers, Department Heads or Associate Deputy Ministers, CIO, and the legal department. The CKO must work with the appropriate groups to develop and periodically review the agency's information KM policy and guidelines.

Risk Analysis

KM Program risk analysis is a process used to determine an agency's vulnerabilities prior to and during the development and deployment of a KM Program.

The CKO should assist staff in assessing KM risks. The risk analysis provides management with informed choices about cost, vulnerabilities, probabilities and solutions.

Summary of CKO Roles and Responsibilities

It is the responsibility of the CEO or Head of the Agency to appoint a CKO. This person must be well versed in all areas of knowledge management and be able to understand the processes and technologies required in support of Decision Support throughout the Agency.

Step 4–KM Program Execution

Phase 1–Advocating

Find your advocate(s). Figure out what their hot button is. Do they want to reduce production costs by 10% over the next two years? Do they want to reduce the amount of paper flow by 20% over the next 3 years? Do they want to increase productivity by 3% over the next year?

Whatever the issue, just make sure there *is* an issue. Once you find the issue then you MUST make sure it is accompanied by a FIXED MEASURING STICK.

Too many KM projects start as touchy feely projects (as I stated earlier) and nobody can figure out if there is ever a Return on Investment. If you know what your target is before you start the outcome is easily measured and quantifiable to everyone.

There is nothing worse than a ship at sea that doesn't know which direction it is going or how long it will take to get there. This makes senior executives very nervous. Best not to make them nervous about KM, especially if they have to eventually commit both time and money. If they are presented, at the beginning of the fiscal year, three projects to spend money on: two with fixed estimates of cost and ROI, and the third is a nebulous KM initiative, you can be certain where the money will get allocated, and it won't be the KM project.

Phase 2–Planning

As with any project, you should be spending at least 50% of your budget and time planning. If you scrimp on the planning stage, you will fail. Don't you just love how blunt I am? I'm blunt because I have been there, survived, and have the T-shirts to prove it. Learn from my mistakes.

Document everything. These will become your own best practices, even if nobody but you ever implements them again. Putting things on paper always forces the entrepreneur to rationalize more than they ever would if they didn't write things down. It also is a good idea to let others read your documents. You know what I'm talking about by now. Yes, the knowledge-sharing thing. Others may provide a lot of insight that will save you time and money (especially on the political side).

This project should be written up just like any other business plan:

- ➤ Mission Statement
- ➤ Budget
- ➤ Timeline
- ➤ Scope
- ➤ Risks
- ➤ Opportunities

➤ Issues

➤ Contingencies

➤ Etc…

And everything should be bound in a wrapper of change management to make sure that scope creep doesn't catch up on you and eat what little money they have assigned for this pilot.

If you have the luxury of a bit of extra time and money, it would also likely prove to be a benefit if you had an external consultant come in and perform a gap analysis towards the end of this phase. Nothing complicated just a simple document that outlines three things:

1. What your vision is
2. Where are you now
3. What is missing that needs to be done to get you to your vision goals

Have them build a table, write down the vision for each aspect of the project, then fill in the blanks.

An independent assessment will also make the management and your advocate(s) a little more comfortable just before they have to put the next round of funding in.

Phase 3–Implementing

Implementation depends on many different things depending on the KM Program you are implementing, such as:

- Timing
- Technology Deployment
- Human Resources
- Training
- Operations
- Support
- etc…

This is when you should be utilizing a true Project Management Framework (such as Rational's Unified Processes or Microsoft's Solution Framework, for examples). These frameworks will provide a huge suite of formal processes that will appear overwhelming. But the fact is, you really just use what you need to and you will find they lend great credibility to the project and provide timelines, milestones and deliverables that are quantifiable for everyone involved. At a minimum, you should be following the project management best practices laid out in the earlier section called Managing a KM Program.

The grand finale of the Implementing phase is the deployment to a select group of early adopters that will provide significant feedback into the development team.

Phase 4–Piloting

Now it is time to move the KM Program into production, but in a selective fashion. Your core development team is no longer the support system, although they may still help on a Tier 2 or 3 support system now and again to assist transition.

Basically, at this phase, you have turned the processes over to management and the technological systems over to the operations teams to manage and maintain. The training department has the training requirements and materials developed into a formal program and the support infrastructure is in place.

All of this is working for the first time in a select area of the organization while you gain confidence, tweak the production aspects and measure your results.

This stage should see the KM program being integrated into the daily workflow. If the KM Program doesn't make it into the daily workflow, then it will likely fizzle and die as soon as the novelty wears off. Both yours and the advocate's jobs are not complete until workflow integration happens.

Phase 5–Institutionalizing

If the results prove worthy of further expansion then this phase sees the KM Program extending into the enterprise.

The biggest change at this stage is the adoption of the KM Program into the business plan of the organization as well as seeing aspects of the program integrated into employee performance reviews.

Now it is recognized as an integral component of the company's success.

But let's get one thing clear at this phase. If you are deploying a tactical solution it may never institutionalize. That is not necessarily a problem. Lot's of tactical programs are brought to life without ever consuming the enterprise or becoming a cornerstone of the business.

As long as the program produced the desired output that the advocate(s) and business owners(s) were hoping to realize then the program was a success.

Appendix A-KM Survey

In this survey there are no right or wrong answers. Use the legend below to determine how to answer the questions:

The "Group" = your working department or section

2	Strongly Agree
1	Agree
0	Don't Know
-1	Disagree
-2	Strongly Disagree
Y	Yes
N	No
DK	Don't Know

1	Does your enterprise have a Chief Knowledge Officer?	Y · N· DK
3	Does your enterprise have a KM Program/System?	Y · N· DK
4	Has your organization recently (past 2 years) gone through downsizing?	Y · N· DK
5	Has your organization recently (past 2 years) been part of a Merger or Acquisition?	Y · N· DK

6	The group understands its business objectives clearly?	2 · 1 · 0 · -1 · -2
7	People follow clear guidelines and instructions about their work	2 · 1 · 0 · -1 · -2
8	Poor performance is dealt with quickly and firmly	2 · 1 · 0 · -1 · -2
9	The group really wants to succeed	2 · 1 · 0 · -1 · -2
10	When opportunities for competitive advantage arise people move decisively to capitalize on them	2 · 1 · 0 · -1 · -2
11	Strategic goals are shared	2 · 1 · 0 · -1 · -2
12	Rewards are clearly understood	2 · 1 · 0 · -1 · -2
13	The group is determined to beat clearly defined competitors or target goals	2 · 1 · 0 · -1 · -2
14	Hitting business goals (i.e., targets) is the single most important thing	2 · 1 · 0 · -1 · -2
15	Projects that are started are usually completed	2 · 1 · 0 · -1 · -2

16	It is clear where one person's job ends and another person's begins	2 · 1 · 0 · -1 · -2
17	People covet what they know and it is difficult at times to get it out of them	2 · 1 · 0 · -1 · -2
18	My immediate supervisor keeps me informed about what is going on.	2 · 1 · 0 · -1 · -2
19	My immediate supervisor does not try to control my work activities.	2 · 1 · 0 · -1 · -2
20	I influence my supervisor's decisions as much as my supervisor influences mine.	2 · 1 · 0 · -1 · -2
21	Workers in my group share information about what is going on.	2 · 1 · 0 · -1 · -2
22	My supervisor lives up to my expectations of him/her.	2 · 1 · 0 · -1 · -2
23	Workers across the organization share information about what is going on.	2 · 1 · 0 · -1 · -2
24	My coworkers take the initiative to solve problems sometimes ignoring rules to do so.	2 · 1 · 0 · -1 · -2
25	My coworkers and I influence one another equally.	2 · 1 · 0 · -1 · -2

26	My coworkers openly discuss what they need of one another.	2 · 1 · 0 · -1 · -2
27	My coworkers live up to my expectations of them.	2 · 1 · 0 · -1 · -2
28	Upper management keeps everyone in the organization informed about what's happening.	2 · 1 · 0 · -1 · -2
29	Upper management encourages workers to take action even when there are no rules to follow.	2 · 1 · 0 · -1 · -2
30	Workers influence upper management in things such as goals, policies, and decisions.	2 · 1 · 0 · -1 · -2
31	There are policies and/or procedures for workers and upper management to clarify their mutual expectations of one another.	2 · 1 · 0 · -1 · -2
32	Upper management lives up to its responsibilities to the workers.	2 · 1 · 0 · -1 · -2
33	The sharing of information across organizational units is open and easy.	2 · 1 · 0 · -1 · -2
34	Workers can get what they need from other organizational units without being discouraged or hampered by rules or procedures.	2 · 1 · 0 · -1 · -2
35	Mechanisms exist whereby basic organizational units influence one another equally in arriving at decisions that impact the units.	2 · 1 · 0 · -1 · -2

36	Basic organizational units clarify or coordinate what each expects of the other(s).	2 · 1 · 0 · -1 · -2
37	Basic organizational units meet their responsibilities to other basic organizational units.	2 · 1 · 0 · -1 · -2
38	It is a formal goal of the organization for all employees to be as open in sharing information as possible.	2 · 1 · 0 · -1 · -2
39	The organization encourages workers to make their own decisions.	2 · 1 · 0 · -1 · -2
40	The organization encourages workers to influence managers.	2 · 1 · 0 · -1 · -2
41	The organization encourages workers to participate in the establishment of their goals and performance objectives.	2 · 1 · 0 · -1 · -2
42	Within the organization, everyone is held responsible for his/her performance and behavior.	2 · 1 · 0 · -1 · -2
43	In your group people share ideas	2 · 1 · 0 · -1 · -2
44	Organizational wide, people share ideas and information	2 · 1 · 0 · -1 · -2
45	When you look for problem-solving information are you more likely to first: choose 1	__ Contact a coworker __ Check corporate systems __ Use outside sources __ Other

46	In the above question, why did you choose the answer you did: choose 1	__ Faster __ Easier __ Better information __ Other
47	Does your company formally reward knowledge sharing?	Y · N· DK

Contributing authors on this section: Vincent Ribiere ribiere@american.edu

0-595-23138-1